At Ease with Images of Art

Also by John Tagliabue

Poems 1942-1958
HARPER BROTHERS, 1959

A Japanese Journal
KAYAK PRESS, 1966

The Buddha Uproar
KAYAK PRESS, 1970

The Doorless Door
MUSHINSHA\GROSSMAN, 1970

The Great Day: Poems 1962-1983
THE ALAMBIC PRESS, 1984

New and Selected Poems: 1942-1997
NATIONAL POETRY FOUNDATION, 1998

An Artist in Rome
accompanied by paintings by Adam Van Doren
KELLY WINTERTON PRESS, 2009

At Ease with Images of Art

Poems
by
John Tagliabue

Edited by Grace Tagliabue
and Henry F. Majewski

At Ease with Images of Art
Poems by John Tagliabue

Edited by Grace Tagliabue & Henry F. Majewski

Copyright ©2014 John Tagliabue
Paperback Black & White Edition

Grace Tagliabue, Publisher
Providence, RI 02906-4491

ISBN-13: 978-1494747183
ISBN-10: 1494747189

All poems in this collection are previously unpublished with the exception
of *Twirling* and *The Sleepwalker*, published in a catalogue of work by the
artist, *Marianna Pineda, Sculpture 1949 to 1996*, The Alabaster Press, Boston,
Massachusetts, 1996.

Cover design includes details from the following works of art:
LE DÉJEUNER SUR L'HERBE, Édouard Manet, 1863, Musée d'Orsay, Paris
BUDDHA, Stone Sculpture, 6th Century, Asian; Chinese, RISD Museum, Providence
THE GOLDFINCH, Carel Fabritius, 1654, Mauritshuis, The Hague
STILL LIFE WITH APPLES, Paul Cézanne, RISD Museum, Providence
Published with permission by the credited museums.

Images included with the poems are published with permission by the numerous
museums. They are credited with the artwork and at the conclusion of the book.

Book Design by Amy Webb
MOCKINGBIRD DESIGN

To artists who inspire–

Being is its own reward for being.

Beauty is its own reward for being.

– J. T.

AT EASE WITH IMAGES OF ART

Poems by
John Tagliabue

TABLE OF CONTENTS:

Preface

Introduction

I.   Poems about the Museum Experience   17

II. Poems from the Museums
     Paris: Louvre   31
                  15th & 16th-Century Art   34
                  17th-Century Art   51
                  18th-Century Art   57
              Musée d'Orsay   66
     Washington D.C.:
                  National Gallery of Art   101
                  The Phillips Collection   116
     New York:
                  Metropolitan Museum of Art   123
     Providence, Rhode Island:
                  Museum of Art
                  Rhode Island School of Design   132

III. Poems Inspired by Favorite Artists   161

IV. 20th-Century Painters & Sculptors in the United States   265

Notes & Museum Credits   289

Re-mind, to find the mind again,
to mine what is most memorable,
valuable.

– J. T.

PREFACE

JOHN WAS A POET. The act of writing a poem was almost a daily necessity and many days he wrote not one but many poems. At times weighty, at times light, at times quizzical his poems flowed out as lyrical notes floating in the breezes. At the same time I imagine he also felt there was a kind of magic, a spirit guiding the act, moving the pen in his hand. He sometimes said that he did not know where a poem had come from or even asked, "Did I write that?" Because of his commitment to poetry I think it follows that he felt the need to respond in words to the visual arts. He loved spending hours in museums, absorbing messages from sculptors, painters, printmakers and other artists, understanding the world through different languages. He also responded to music but less with words, more by dancing, improvising with body gestures, interpreting sounds that mesmerized him. As the poem which gives us the title for this small selection from many of John's unpublished poems suggests "Let reading and writing be a form of bowing, of gaining strength" he felt a reverence for art and its power to teach, to guide and even to restore a belief in the sacredness of life. I was delighted when our dear friend, Henry Majewski, suggested we make a selection of John's poems inspired by his travels and his love of art. We believe the poems will speak for themselves, as John explains in these three lines:

> He could not cross the bridge
> Until he wrote a poem
> The poem being the bridge.

Grace Tagliabue

INTRODUCTION TO
At Ease with Images of Art

THE POET JOHN TAGLIABUE AND HIS WIFE GRACE traveled extensively during his career as a professor and writer. They spent time in many countries including the Middle and Far East where John taught literature and practiced the art of poetry. His favorite destinations in every major city were always the museums of art. He wrote many poems about paintings and other artworks including sculpture, frescoes and stained glass. Some of these poems have been published in previous books of poetry or magazines and catalogues: for this collection we have therefore concentrated on the poems which have not been published before and were written during his years of retirement when he lived in Providence, Rhode Island, and traveled mainly to Western Europe. [1]

John's beautiful and perceptive poems about art can be situated in a long tradition of ekphrastic poetry from Homer to the present. The scholar James Heffernan has studied many aspects of this approach to poetry in his illuminating work entitled *Museum of Words*.[2] There he defines this poetic practice as essentially the verbal representation of a visual representation. In the French tradition this mode of writing is referred to as a "transposition d'art." A transposition from one artistic medium to another based on the idea of fundamental relationships and even unity between the arts, or in Baudelaire's famous phrase a correspondence between the arts. Many excellent studies have appeared in the last fifty years on this subject including the poet John Hollander's work entitled *The Gazer's Spirit: Poems Speaking to Silent Works of Art* in which he illustrates and analyzes this poetic practice with many beautiful examples of poems that enter into a dialogue with a work of art.[3]

The concept of the spirit of the poet looking is particularly appropriate to the approach John implements. In his poems he most often celebrates the work he admires and discovers in the experience of writing the poem that he, the poet, has been spiritually enriched by the act of looking and writing. The dialogue between him and the artist is not a confrontation or a desire to improve on the image through words, but an attempt to reach the spiritual essence of the work and express it verbally, thus giving it a new form of understanding and value. In other forms of ekphrastic poetry the poet might attempt to recreate the poem through description or use its images to symbolize an idea or a theme. Some poets create a narrative based on details from the painting, and it becomes a springboard to project their desires and imagination. John enters into a communication or even communion with the work of art. Sometimes with the artist or with the subject of the painting that often results in a heightened sense of the spirituality and beauty of the work.

The text has been organized to provide an overview of the poet's achievement: we begin with a series of poems in which he presents his method, his approach to a work of art in the many museums he visited and loved. After this introductory section we have organized the poems first according to some of the major museums he visited in Paris, such as the Louvre and the Musée d'Orsay. Then we move to the United States, including Washington, New York and finally Providence, Rhode Island where he resided during his last years and where he grew to love the fine museum at the School of Design. Following this section on the museums, we have placed a series of poems devoted to some of John's favorite artists, such as Cézanne, van Gogh and Rembrandt: they are presented in alphabetical order.

In conclusion is a series of poems dealing with 20th-century American artists, including the Maine artists Marsden Hartley and John Marin; Betty Woodman, a ceramic artist and Marianna Pineda, a sculptor, complete the selection.

At the end of each poem we have placed the generally accepted titles of each art work and have added the date and location of the work as accurately as was possible. We have made a choice of reproductions to indicate the range of John's experience with the world of art.

Permissions to reproduce the illustrations of art works have been graciously authorized and listed at the conclusion of the book.

Henry F. Majewski

Professor Emeritus of French Studies
Brown University

NOTES

1. All poems in this collection are unpublished with the exception of *Twirling* and *The Sleepwalker*, published in a catalogue of work by artist, Marianna Pineda. Hills, Patricia & Tagliabue, John. *Marianna Pineda, Sculpture 1949 to 1996.* The Alabaster Press, Boston, MA, 1996.

2. Heffernan, James A. W. *Museum of Words: the Poetics of Ekphrasis from Homer to Ashberry.* Chicago: University of Chicago Press. 1993.

3. Hollander, John. *The Gazer's Spirit: Poems Speaking to Silent Works of Art.* Chicago: University of Chicago Press. 1995.

I

POEMS AND NOTES
about the museum experience

*We who have lived quite a few years and who have
gone often from museum room to museum room, from
Blake to Giacometti, from Constable to Andy Warhol,
know we can somehow take it, all the changes of mind
and mood and culture; what it will make of us the
complete works will show.
More myths, more metaphors…*

Buddha
STONE SCULPTURE
6th Century – Asian; Chinese
RISD Museum, Providence

Let reading and writing be a form of bowing,
of gaining strength

I feel so at ease with Images of art that
        console
or give some hope centrality in their wisdom,
        why do not
some artists care for me via their compositions, my
        centrality?
even the wildest ancient and modern artists do
        (Aeschylus,
Dostoyevsky, etc.); Buddha knew suffering, sickness,
        death, but
the anonymous 6th century Chinese grey stone Image
        of him is
smiling; benevolent well centered meditating
        knows
something he thinks we ought to know, so as well
        as sitting
he wandered to teach; the stone mason who made
        this head man
(probably with all his difficulties) succeeded in
        conveying
his calm, constructing his survivor's wisdom.

There is some insurance, assurance

A museum always gives me a good destination
      in life, at least
for the exercise of a walk; one can't always be
      sure that the
Muse and I will converse like mad in love or
      calm in
contemplation; but then one cannot be sure of most
      things, though
what urged music and design in nature once
      if you are
stirring you can often be up to it. Mozart's notes
      await a
conductor. Monet and Corot await the breath
      of your
life, the brush stroke of your ardor,
      imagination

Colorful Recognition Scenes Galore

I can believe it –
you are all there waiting for me –
pictures in the museums of the world, Washington, D. C.,
          Seattle, Louvre,
Rome, Tokyo and everywhere, waiting with all your
          vibrations and messages
in tact, in form, waiting for me to come, commune,
          pay my entrance fee, soul,
give myself away, have dialogue with you, like those
          young lovers in the Balcony Scene.
I look up and write it down, you understand, and when I leave
          I feel the whole museum is
          smiling, is satisfied.

Seeing as a way of Sailing

> While I can still see I must see,
>   I must see
> while I can still walk, wow, I must
>   walk, I will,
> while I continue my rites of passage
>   I must write,
> I do, while I can still dream I
>   really see,
> while I must travel from country to
>   country, we set
>   out to see.

On the occasion of meeting a great poem or a great painting

One goes through hundreds of rooms where they (the paintings) and I
      have not as
exactly and as fully as possible arrived and one realizes that's natural,
      frequent, as with
people or city streets, time that does not seem like your Awakening.
      But then a Sunflower
by Blake or van Gogh comes into or out of our lives, it grows
      wider, it has
the Unnameable as the Center and within that the sun and our solar
      system and our genesis.
We generate more fables, more bibles, after this Event. The
      vibrations in the seeds
of the prayers of the saints from everywhere and all time are
      contained in the darkness
      and time of that union.

Braque at Constructive Work

Do you mind if I take you apart,
        for the
heaven and music and mathematical pleasure
        of it,
if I who love you and painting area by
        area
devise divisions and textures for the love of
        them and
you? I will take you apart to show my
        heart, to
make playful and re-constructive my art,
        I will
canvas you, construct you so neatly,
        subtle and
subdued so as to edify a contemplation.

Give praise to the Immortal

Ascending ascending ascending
again and again – for the millionth time? –
      going up
some stairs to see some works of art, one works
      at it and
after walking many streets in New York London
      Paris etc.
mortal age being what it is one finds the going
      much slower;
slow? fast? pain difficulty ease? what does
      that matter?
one is a senior symbolist; all moments give
      freedom to the immortal.

Burning all over

A painting does plenty of talking but
  it's not loud
and as I change and return to it I find out
  different colors
entertainments messages from it. You can put
  your ear to a
sea shell and hear the past. And quietly you can
  to all sorts of
tones and philosophies and personal profundities implied
  from different
scenes in or out of museums or churches or private
  places of prayer.
A painting, it doesn't have to be by El Greco or van Gogh,
  it can be by
Chardin or Seurat or Modigliani, others too, can send
  you up in
flames and when you descend and shift your weight to the
  other leg
it can be calm and endless in its energy supply. So
  if you
need a boost or an adventure or at least partly wise
  conversation
you can go learning all over to many good paintings.

Dialogue:
The Anonymous lover and the particular Muse;
or   Are we as complete as can be?

You should put your name on it, Picasso does;
suppose Picasso signed his name Cro-Magnon Man or
Pithecanthropus Erectus signed his name Miró would it
make any difference to the painting? it's there for
the asking, the painting, on wall or canvas
or in the air; signed on the waters of the world;
the words become fishes; suppose you sign your name
on every bottom corner of every church in the world
would that make your children more religious?
what are you talking about? you didn't make all
the churches in the world, you didn't even completely
      make one epic or one
      SUMMA THEOLGICA.

Visionaries come momentarily to the surface

I have seen millions of paintings, large,
       small, modern,
ancient; my eyes are now closed as I sit
       in the corner of a
Special Parisian Exhibit. Murmuring, babbling,
       necessary in streams
and in museum crowds, under the Sistine Ceiling
       or here between
Fra Angelico and Bonnard paintings. Murmurings
       blending together
like colors in an impressionist or post-impressionist
       painting; Sisley,
Signac, Vuillard. A variety of undecipherable
       languages,
Relatives are talking after their death, People are talking
       in their sleep.

We contain multitudes

When I think of it,
that they were all
writing to me, these
painters in all the
museums that I
have seen and spoken to,
I realize we are not
at a loss for words but
for words and color and
love we are found.

Largesse with thousands of Pictures

Am I in Paris
or in the world of thought, of images
        betokening gifts,
betokening stirring treasures understandings
        gifted practitioners of
the soul? here it is in a universal Consciousness
        where we exist.
Exist? If we give the gift outright to these, our
        love increases colorfully,
            the Louvre is large.

II POEMS FROM THE MUSEUMS

PARIS:

The Louvre

*The idea that many many artists had – Apollinaire,
Gertrude Stein, Hemingway, Picasso, Stravinsky and
on and on – of Paris as the center of the art world,
as the symbol of the freedom of the imagination's
expression…that continues to make a big difference…
it alerts us to fantasy and fact. The fact that these
fancies occur often in broad daylight in one of the
visually most beautiful cities in the world also makes
a big difference. Our fortune.*

Greek, Hellenistic
WINGED VICTORY OF SAMOTHRACE
200-190 BC
Louvre, Paris

Suggestions from Samothrace

Faith can move mountains,
the winged notions of the artist in love
          with wings,
liberty, motion, striding can make of a
          large large strong
stone a fluttering, a Winged Victory;
          such striding of
the Imagination, the strong wind stirring
          the tunic of the
forward moving music body of the heroine
          prepares for Hope;
          Advance.

15TH &16TH-CENTURY ART AT THE LOUVRE

I'm waiting too

As a matter of fact, not morbid
     the Crucifix
is central. And you, my brother,
     Fra Angelico,
are factual faithful. No melodrama;
     no sentimentality.
It cannot be avoided. Man's disobedience.
     Man's cruelty.
Suffering. Plain facts – as complex as
     can be.
Earthly being can be transcended then
     what you will see
     tell me.

Fra Angelico
FRESCO OF CALVARY
1440
Louvre, Paris

The Fortune Teller

The plump intelligent harmonious
Fortune Teller holds his hand, feels his palm,
eyes smiling the handsome fellow, mature in youth
          and wealth and comfort,
elegant and with fine clothes, androgynous beauty,
          and a plume in his hat,
she is glad to be in touch with him, receive his
          money and foretell
his luscious future pride and adventures.

Caravaggio
THE FORTUNE TELLER
1594
Louvre, Paris

Venus and Cupid asleep discovered by a Satyr

No wonder all the leaves in the forest are trembling
　　　　excited
by his desire for naked ripe rich in repose
　　　　golden
harmonious Italian Venus; his desire can make
　　　　energy
flow through the roots of trees; the dream sight of her
　　　　strengthens his
　　　　proclivities.

Antonio Correggio
VENUS, SATYR AND CUPID
1527
Louvre, Paris

Domenico Ghirlandaio
PORTRAIT OF AN OLD MAN WITH A YOUNG BOY
1490
Louvre, Paris

Portrait of an Old Man
a very young boy in a red cap is looking up at him

Some limited people might say,
        Grandfather,
that your huge bumpy nose is weird
        or funny,
but I, your visiting most admiring grandson,
        know better,
love, adore, your noble kind strong good
        character,
even when you, O my inspiration and wisdom,
        are bodily gone
your goodness will have made for me hope
        and
knowledge that the world can be good, perfect,
        ti ringrazio.

Can anyone do that now, imagine the faces like those of the two women created in this painting, the quality and soul that they reveal, the health of harmony they reveal? Nowhere anywhere near this quiddity, this blessed knowledge, being, imagined and created in most 20th century art; a big philosophic subject to reason about. But now I'll look at some more Italian Renaissance paintings. What they knew - Duccio, Cimabue, Giotto, Leonardo - far far from the wasteland of much in the modern world.

Leonardo da Vinci
THE VIRGIN AND CHILD WITH ST. ANNE
1508
Louvre, Paris

The Genius calmly ascends again

The little lamb seems pleased
(and not professional or touristy) as he looks up
        at the child smiling
who touches him and looks up at his mother, she is gentle
        pleased harmonious as
all Heaven in the lap of her mother Anne, it is music,
        it is an ascent
from earth to heaven and at the same time from eternity
        to time, ascent
from Anne and Mary to all that they behold

A dense crowd in sandals, blue jeans, short and long skirts, from all countries – they huddle in variety and with cameras in a semi-circle around her. In different parts of this large room are many small and huge pictures reflected in her protective glass and tourist guides are shouting explanations in different languages.

A Model for the Sphinx

Monday at the Louvre again
millions at the Louvre again,
flash flash flash and the Mona Lisa remains
       perfectly still
how many millions from Japan, China, India,
       all of Europe, North and
South America are taking pictures of her, more
       crowded than Macy's
Basement during a Christmas sale, she's perfectly
       still and sort of
smiling, some repeat for centuries she is sort of
       enigmatic, her
author was complex, she reminds me of my
       aunts, as a
matter of fact they are smiling and enigmatic in heaven;
       she remains perfectly still.

Portrait of Mona Lisa called Giaconda

Well, you can come to a snap judgment,
        interpretation,
fix her in 10,000 phrases, and yourselves,
        I am addressing
you mysterious and smiling and smirking and laughing
        and often
snapshot taking visitors, some are shouting for
        lost cousins,
some are taking flash pictures of her, the
        MONA LISA
behind a glass of many reflections, she is
        as calm
as ever, as enigmatic as everybody; the
        position
of her hands has been studied by a million,
        more scholars,
East, West; tourists, some in their shorts,
        some in it seems
bathing suits, tourists of all sizes and shapes,
        from Hong Kong and
everywhere, many carrying knapsacks and joking
        with each other,
have arrived at a destination, the most
        frequented picture
in the Louvre; a destiny; I hope it's a genuine
        Renaissance for them.

Leonardo da Vinci
MONA LISA, *detail*
1503-1506
Louvre, Paris

Madonna of the Grotto
with St. John and Christ as children and an archangel

    In the dark grotto
    who is blessing whom, who is
          praying to
    whom? It is a mutual admiration circle
          of esoteric
    protectors and champions; we have to hide in the
          dark sometimes,
    to whisper prayers in greatest and most distant
          intimacy, have to
    realize, be mystified, find each other in a
          most secret grotto
          of all chiaroscuro.

Leonardo da Vinci
The Virgin of the Rocks
1483
Louvre, Paris

Portrait of a Young Princess

Naturally at a loss for words
that's why Pisanello's paintings were needed
or small green piselli (peas) or flowers
to please, to be exotic precise, picturesque, but
here is a precious young girl in profile, surrounded
by little flowers like lights in a dark private carnival
very private, profile and flowering of poetry,
O Pisanello, you tease us, O
princess, you will make me
want to return to the earth
forever. Plus I see a few
exotic butterflies in the dark.

Antonio Pisanello
PORTRAIT OF GINEVRA D'ESTE
1440
Louvre, Paris

Andrea Mantegna
Saint Sebastian
1480
Louvre, Paris

Ruins. Difficulties. Disasters.
And a maintenance of faith

Brave somber
Mantegna maintaining poise, hope, and a great
    awareness of tragic
suffering maintains his moral equilibrium as he
    looks into his
heart and writes, sees the young tortured standing against
    a column St. Sebastian,
against a cliff below clouds, shot through with agonies
    arrows, he wonders,
we wonder, about man's cruelty to man.
    Gravity; Greyness;
the tall standing highness of faith and adoration
    with sorrow endures.

Raphael
ST. GEORGE FIGHTING THE DRAGON
1505
Louvre, Paris

A 16th century victory continues

Youthful Raphael with his perfect stroke and
    sense of color, calm,
a young genius; youthful armored St. George
    riding on a heavy
gallant white horse, the soldier saint's cape
    flying, his feet
firmly in the stirrups, the supporting horse rearing,
    The swashbuckling youth
with his strong arm and curved high held sword
    about to slash the
dragon, the fabulous beast shivers like a
    dying bat, the Italian Umbrian
scene is idyllic perfect; the young author has won
    the war; has finished the painting.

Performance by Raphael and Others

St. Michael
youthful ballet dancer
en pointe the other graceful leg in the air,
winged, even better than Nureyev, while part of
       the sky is ablaze,
steps fearlessly bravely on the wrinkled distorted
       snake-like slithering demon,
the graceful unworried winged saint with his spear
       kills the withering beast
while a dazed Japanese tour group is very amazed;
       some take photographs.

Raphael
St. Michael Victorious
1518
Louvre, Paris

17TH-CENTURY ART AT THE LOUVRE

Rembrandt van Rijn
Saint Matthew Inspired by an Angel
1661
Louvre, Paris

St. Matthew Inspired by an Angel

Now I remember this – do you still hear it?
　　　when the door opened
and as quietly as possible, as quietly as
　　　the angel walked
into the room and near the ear of St. Matthew
　　　quietly quietly
whispered – remember the Holy Dove descending,
　　　remember the
friend ascending; the word is quieter than a bird.
　　　The marks by
the sea, the remarks on the page, disappear, but
　　　the need to hear
recurs; remember when you walked perfectly into
　　　the room and
you said to me what I cannot forget what we
　　　must all repeat.

Le Boeuf Ecorché

So here is a vast epic –
      he
huge once a vital power grazing
      hung up
his hind legs distended, his open
      once vital
revealing carcass extended, here are
      books of
Revelation, so each beast, so each
      word, of
God is more than Aeschylus and Testaments
      can say.

Rembrandt van Rijn
LE BOEUF ECORCHÉ
1655
Louvre, Paris

La Dentellière

> I give full attention, I give detail,
> > I think of my
> farmer grandmother, mother of 11, carefully
> > making lace,
> praying to God. She herself is a detail,
> > a star, a
> pensive one in absolute attention which is prayer.
> > The dim
> light around her, and on her brow, and on the lace
> > makes
> possible, pattern makes possible, this pattern.

Johannes Vermeer
LA DENTELLIÈRE
1669
Louvre, Paris

Vermeer too casting modestly some light
on the Astronomical subject

The Vermeer Astronomer tender touching regarding,
        he in his large
robe, dark sky blue, like a careful Prospero,
        touching upon the
countries of the Turning Mystery as if they were Braille,
        he related to stars
and their energies, in curious and cautious meditation.
        The light of the sun
comes through the study window to enlighten part of
        the globe and
the brow of the pensive attending one.

Johannes Vermeer
THE ASTRONOMER
1668
Louvre, Paris

56

18TH & 19TH-CENTURY ART AT THE LOUVRE

David's Vast Panorama of Napoleon's Coronation in Notre Dame

Bold Assertive Aggressive
egomaniac Napoleon staging himself on the
      world stage
takes the crown from the Pope and crowns
      himself and Josephine,
dazzles himself, dazes millions. Little
      proud Corsican
like other famous political leaders ends
      up in dust.

Jacques-Louis David
CONSECRATION OF THE EMPEROR NAPOLEON I
AND CORONATION OF THE EMPRESS JOSEPHINE, DECEMBER 4, 1804
1806-07
Louvre, Paris

Delacroix's Liberty Leading the People

Naked triumph
boldness upsurge on going
boldness and breasts showing, the French flag
     held high,
onward over repeated centuries of causes and
     massacres,
revolts and cries for justice and revenge,
     the fury of
outlashing long suppressed released, all kinds and
     ages in frustration
in frenzy, in righteous or blind fury in smoke and
     gunfire in
insistence and confusion keeps going. And when
     will it
end and how will it end?

Eugène Delacroix
LIBERTY LEADING THE PEOPLE
1830
Louvre, Paris

Théodore Géricault
THE RAFT OF THE MEDUSA
1819
Louvre, Paris

Géricault's The Raft of the Medusa

One wreck or another, large, small,
one massacre or another, one bombardment or
        another, one
shipwreck, body wreck, one world, a huddle of
        agonies,
a concentration of outcries, pains, disasters
        abound,
we are bound to the battered cross, bound
        for torment,
see how history tortures, how large enterprises
        falter, see
how Adam falls with his crew, there in the
        vortex shipwreck
of our contention and discontent, heavily and in chaos
        we struggle for salvation.

Jean-Auguste Ingres
OEDIPUS EXPLAINS THE RIDDLE OF THE SPHINX
1814
Louvre, Paris

Ingres' Oedipus Confronting the Enigma

Enigma   enigma   enigma
within Oedipus as he confronts
the enigma within the enigma of the
Enigma...naked as a new born child or
youth he inquires puzzled by destiny,
confronting winged beast or woman
concerning a winged enigma; if
the question were not
enigmatic the answers
would astound
beyond this
life

Jean-Antoine Watteau
PIERROT, ALSO KNOWN AS GILLES
1718
Louvre, Paris

Watteau's Pierrot

Cast
into the world
like a white satin strip
blown to this scene   this stage
from far from where and for what purpose?
startling   central   belonging not to this
not to that   suspended in stasis
in sadness   like a costume
like a puppet for a time
abused   abandoned

Gilles of the small eyes
after years of weeping   he of the satin costume
accustomed to being in this life out of place

the large eye of the donkey   he approaching
only partly seen   he seems to
understand the plight of the
injured one   he
who is paid to
play the Fool

PARIS:

Musée d'Orsay

*I have written notes and poems suggested by drawings
– but mostly by paintings; perhaps I especially respond
to messages, vibrancies, emotional effect from colors?*

Nature morte à la Soupière

Well, Soupière,
You have your French ceramic white, blue,
      green, yellow
design on your closed lid, you are near
      with ease
this sort of country cousins, apples, plums,
      but now
I want to mostly call attention to you, large
      Soupière,
you will possibly warm delicious soup,
      I take it
personally the way I do every sip, every
      breath,
every glance; what am I here for if not
      to be
nourished? if not to be very intimate
      personal?

Paul Cézanne
Still Life with a Soupière
1877
Musée d'Orsay, Paris

Paul Cézanne
MONT SAINTE-VICTOIRE
1890
Musée d'Orsay, Paris

Mont Sainte-Victoire, Cézanne and so forth (1890 scene)

It was his Mt. Fuji,
but more appropriate for him, less a
        matter of
accumulated Tradition and accumulated ashes,
        it was in
a more gentle Mediterranean climate and terrain;
        accumulated
and growing devotion makes us strengthen
        the sacred,
gives us a direction for worship and
        ascendency.

La Femme à la Cafetière

My morning coffee maker,
little token, I hear you bubble, murmur
    in the morning,
bubble up, to wake me up, you served my
    mother who
drank it dark coffee, helpful assistant,
    every day for
more than 90 years. You are not exactly
    on an altar
but you serve our purposes so
    as to stimulate
more arguments, more or less
    emotion,
more motions than one knows to make
    decisions,
purposes; sphinxes in the desert have
    nothing on us.

Paul Cézanne
La Femme à la Cafetière
1890/98
Musée d'Orsay, Paris

Portrait de Mme. Cézanne

Sit still, will you,
Become my idol, everybody's idol,
representative of
      a particular mystery,
      actual and ideal;
I deal with you as I would a mountain
of oranges
      but this time we are
      tones and poems of
      monumental blue
      and green.

Paul Cézanne
PORTRAIT OF MME. CÉZANNE
1885
Musée d'Orsay, Paris

Les Baigneurs

And so the Cézanne nudes do not intrude with
      angst,
free of desire they clarify infinity as trees do
      as clouds do.
What coolness refreshes, informs us of our purest
      nascence; at play, imagined.

Paul Cézanne
BAIGNEURS
1890-92
Musée d'Orsay, Paris

NOTES: Cezanne

*I think we love him too (Cézanne) because he did not whine in
solitude, strong worker composer that he was; he was not looking for
a subject, found one here, there democratic aristocrat, did not need a
king or Napoleon, an almost secluded bridge in the woods would do,
its reflection in the almost still stream in the darkness. Just make
a sign of pleasure, of respect, that's sacred work enough. Take it or
leave it. If you can not make something of solitude, a strength, a
private civilization, how can you have a real dialogue or a slightly
decent society?*
I am looking at Cézanne's "Le pont de Maincy près de Melun" 1879

Paul Cézanne
LE PONT DE MAINCY PRÈS DE MELUN
1879
Musée d'Orsay, Paris

72

Charles Cottet's "Le Cirque"

Curious people with curious hats are
       leaning in
and looking at what is or might be going on in
       a curious
circus. A tiger is swishing his curious triumphant
       tail; a fat
gentleman is preening his active moustache; a
       woman in gilded
tights on the flying trapeze is taking her chances;
       an elephant is
lifting his triumphant nose; a clown is
       emerging from a
cannon with a dainty flower in his mouth;
       a bewildered
visitor is touching his girlfriend's thigh.

Charles Cottet
LE CIRQUE
1915
Musée d'Orsay, Paris

Et l'or de leur corps

Don't clarify, Descartes, don't oversimplify
      Logic,
intellect; respect the mystery of streams, of
      fruit
of our destiny here or in Tahiti; see there is a
      Bhagavad-Gita
in everything; an unutterable mystery that is
      the source of
all religious quests. Requests before Tahitian
      flowers;
here two nude dark women in darkness before
      red flowers.
We bow; and no Descartes or theology can explain
      that which
attracts God to islands or the vital.

Paul Gauguin
Et l'or de leur corps
1901
Musée d'Orsay, Paris

Les meules jaunes ou La maison blonde

What a mountain or temple of a haystack wide
      warm that
these 1889 Gauguin farm girls work by is enough to
      make us
sleepy and dreamy a ladder leans against
      a tree, an
emotional Spanish son visiting the Painting with
      his loud
talkative mother begins an argument; they leave;
      I return to
the Haystack; it has become even more a source of
      wonder and quietness.

Paul Gauguin
LES MEULES JAUNES OU LA MAISON BLONDE
1889
Musée d'Orsay, Paris

In this 1898 Gauguin scene another figure too is almost
Hidden in the distance in the quiet Eden of green
And darkness

Paul Gauguin
Un Cheval Blanc
1898
Musée d'Orsay, Paris

Un Cheval Blanc

A bluish greenish horse called "un cheval blanc"
        bends his
god-like sleepy head dazed to drink in the secluded
        Tahitian darker
bluish stream; what dream is this I am participating
        in? Gauguin
was here; he left his green and blue, some other
        hints, designs
to make us drink and dream; I see in the
        distance bewildered
Paul is gone having performed his sacredness,
        I see a nude
rider on a brownish horse about to climb
        a bit, to leave.

Le Repas

Wanting to worship much much much
    we go to
this bowl of coconut milk, this cluster of
    reddish bananas,
this fruit, well formed, greenish, yellow;
    we go in
silence to these brothers and sisters seated before
    the
offerings, this presentation of fruit; Gauguin
    wishes
to see, to say, protect this fruition, this offering,
    this fruit.

Paul Gauguin
LE REPAS
1891
Musée d'Orsay, Paris

At the end of the day in the Paris d'Orsay Museum

I have gone as far as I can go today,
    I have
gotten to Gauguin, je suis fatigué,
    I need
Tahiti of the soul, never seen on land or sea,
    but seen
again and again is the wish fulfillment of this
    saint Paul,
poor banker, rich painter, generous composer
    of colors.
Now I must sleep, dream myself to sleep, before
    he and I sing again.

Édouard Manet
LE DÉJEUNER SUR L'HERBE
1863
Musée d'Orsay, Paris

80

Manet's Le Déjeuner sur l'herbe

It's good to have a
        nude model,
        to remember our humanity,
        to sense its harmony of the spheres,
        to realize our Imagination's ideal;
in the shade to be nourished, relax, repose, recreate
        the nudity and beauty, the order and
        proportions of what we admire; be teased
        and pleased into eternity by the
        factual figure, as fabulous as we
        can get, as we can give:
fruit, a cool stream, acquaintance or Maenad; memory
        from Eden; don't forget desire, contemplation,
        art and the picnic, flowers,
        leaves are natural music.

Manet's Le Déjeuner sur l'herbe
or
What was all the fuss about?

The intellectuals, French, at a picnic,
  relaxed,
with plenty of opinions, some bread and
  fruit,
the 2 knowledgeable men with beards,
  and a relaxed
naked woman, are perhaps discussing
  with some logic
and self-regard art and politics. All
  is well
composed by detached and interested Manet.

 It took me a long time and many ups and downs and quite a few escalators to get back to this Picnic. An important thing – a Nude and a Theory. And "Déjeuner sur l'herbe". Plus near her cool derriere a basket with fruit. A roll, a blue spotted mantle, a straw hat; a cool perspective at the center and behind the discussing group. Later groups of professors with clothed undergraduates will explain at length and with slides the forerunners of Impressionism. But now it's time for me to sit in a comfortable straw chair. The undisturbed model for Master Manet looks notices with my imagination for years at millions stopping to look at the picnic. Professors will pick it apart and have some crumbs for the hungry or not students. Composure and a grand and cool Composition. A satisfaction for its Author and for millions from Japan, Australia, USA and elsewhere. One never knows how many bees a flower will attract or how many people will sing at your opera.

It's time for me to leave this picnic.

Grosse mer à Etretat

Well, we're doing a little group gathering
      Sightseeing
while we can, cold cold grey morning, and in
      our friendly way
not far from a stark high I guess indifferent
      High Cliff
confronting thunderous dramatic high rhythmical
      culminating
Splashing profoundly Active Ocean Waves,
      we prize
our precious sentiments our sense of seeing
      hearing the
picturesque, It (what? who? where?) is
      Indifferent?
our coats and thoughts help keep us warm;
      Manet is
not indifferent as he regards It and us,
      he is
like you, my intimate reader, a poet.

Édouard Manet
GROSSE MER À ETRETAT
1869
Musée d'Orsay, Paris

*Scenes in all seasons at all moments of day-or-eternity of the
Façade of the Cathedral of Rouen*

Now the façade of a cathedral can
   dissolve
like a dew drop or the changing expression
   of your
ever present face. A snow drop dissolves
   but then
I wonder about the doors of the Memory, the
   doors of the Memory!

            Claude Monet
          Rouen Cathedral Series
              1892-1895
          Musée d'Orsay, Paris

Facing up
to a façade of this
a façade of that
and all in changing Monet light
helps dramatize depict a history of
   a philosophy

To respect Monet and the Book of Changes

At different times of day, say, sunset,
   any time,
at different stages of light of life, I prayed,
   I looked at
you, Rouen Cathedral or haystack; our
   destinies were
arranged. Vibrations palpitate, it is not too late to
   enlighten each
   other again.

Notes

*A group of 5 Japanese young women listen to a plump small
Japanese teacher praising Monet, they make a semi-circle
around him and bow. Monet as we saw in his Giverney
home and in many places and ways so the give and take goes
on. As I've said elsewhere the Japanese are geniuses at sleep
and transformations and art. I inevitably interrupt my
contemplation of these paintings to talk with a very pretty
Osaka girl; and briefly I give her my Japan life story. She and
her Naiads leave and I return to the dark blue purple green
water scenes of bearded sage Monet.*
*The world is smaller than an atom and larger than our
thought. I learned these paintings by heart many years ago.
One to my left is of an empty rowboat, Japanese, oddly up in
a corner an area of pond grass, some tree leaves covering part
of it, and dark blue water on the lower right. In Chinese and
Japanese Buddhist influenced paintings there is much "mushin"
or "emptiness"; it takes place lightly in the spaciousness of the
inner self.…Then I turn my gaze to the Nymphéas – to Water
Lilies and the reflections of a Weeping Willow; naming colors
– blues, purples, greens – remind me that a color is a color
and not a paraphrase or name of a color. So narrative and
explanation can never equal the Poem Itself or the Painting
Itself. But prose and paraphrase sometimes can please and help.*

Le Mont Kolsaas en Norvège....1895

– after many hours of writing in the Musée d'Orsay

Breathing out, expiration, advancing Inspiration, Awakening

I, the scribbler, am beginning to fade out
    at last
temporarily in front of this mountain of
    slightly
bluish and pinkish snow by Master Mind
    Monet,
it has a soft quality of dusk and glory,
    silence,
that induces rest, sleep, contemplation,
    Awakening.

Claude Monet
LE MONT KOLSAAS EN NORVÈGE
1895
Musée d'Orsay, Paris

La Coquille

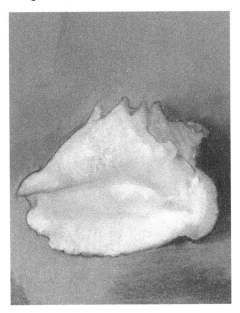

In a trance
tired after sea voyages
staring at you I begin to hear
you, soft soft a moment now,
you temple of secrets and revelations,
you shell more ancient than the Sphinx

I listen again and again to you

you take me in   I am lost

we are   everywhere

Odilon Redon
LA COQUILLE, *detail*
1912
Musée d'Orsay, Paris

87

Bal du Moulin de la Galette

Renoir is throwing a party –
it takes time – it takes many people –
it takes a garden, music, France of course, it takes
many colors, embracing, talking, activity galore, it takes
much flickering, joy, vibrancy, hats, reflections in glasses,
shimmering on silk, on dresses, it takes abundance of
leaves, summer, joy, it takes
varied vital enlightenment
of pleasure.

Pierre-Auguste Renoir
BAL DU MOULIN DE LA GALETTE
1876
Musée d'Orsay, Paris

Nu Couché vu de dos

Down to earth does not belittle in Renoir,
   the plump rosey behind,
backside, back, shoulders, pastoral background refreshed
   by memories of Eden,
reverence and rainbows make us play, desire to caress,
   to be known;
simply the fact of flowers, women, skies, lovely scenes,
   breasts, vacations
of the sensual success, celebrations; to love the figure in the
round
   warmly gives earth
   its welcome.

Pierre-Auguste Renoir
Nu Couché vu de Dos
1885
Musée d'Orsay, Paris

89

Fraises

Renoir
what large strawberries you depict, so ripe so very ripeness
so very cared for
        cherished touched up
most lightly, nipples and sugar and lemon and all, light,
caresses;
        that which does not cloy,
        not destroy,
that which like the perfect strawberry teaches saints about
god; you
        provide a whole bowl
        of them, fresh.

Pierre-Auguste Renoir
Fraises
1905
Seen at the Musée d'Orsay, in the collection of Musée de l'Orangerie, Paris

Femme nue couchée (Gabrielle)

The lineaments of satisfied desire without apocalyptic fanfare or
    stress or strain,
without demands without possessiveness but just perfect in plumpness
    and ripeness, a
summer of a body, nude naturally, Renoir supernaturally; extended
    on the couch
you extend our reveries without worries. I prefer the large curve of your hip
    to the mountains of Canada.

Pierre-Auguste Renoir
FEMME NUE COUCHÉE
1906-1907
Seen at the Musée d'Orsay, in the collection of Musée de l'Orangerie, Paris

Henri Rousseau
LA GUERRE OU LA CHEVAUCHÉE DE LA DISCORDE
1894
Musée d'Orsay, Paris

War or the Cavalcade of Discord

Beyond fucking
beyond slaughter
beyond success and failure
beyond the craven ravens croaking
beyond cut off hands, pieces of flesh in
          the mouths of
bleeding birds, fury and fur in words,
          beyond Hiroshima
and slaughter and more slaughter and
          another chopped lamb
beyond all the sad faces of the tortured
          and the witnesses
of the keepers of the prison of the procession
          of sinners
the sign of the cross the signature
          of the
visiting One; visitor: "they know not what
          they do."

Seen-and-created

She is dark
and she is so much in the dark
and she is darkly naked though a little
      light defines
some of her curves as she plays a dark flute
      under a
small round moon and charms a host of,
      a chorus of,
snakes as they bend in various ways to the sound
      of notes,
poems, the tall stiff Henri Rousseau tropical
      grass is
at full attention, the wide leaves outdo
      Walt Whitman,
the greenish blue rippling wide river in
      the jungle
goes perfectly well with some half hidden
      blossoming
flowers; an inquisitive partly dim fish
      presents itself to
      the pageantry.

Henri Rousseau
The Snake Charmer
1907
Musée d'Orsay, Paris

Small scenes by Seurat

These pleasures in the park, in the
        stream,
in the shade of the summer trees, these dots
        of signs of
love by Seurat, these parasols, these dressed
        or nude
visitors to our dream, these hats, designs,
        circles or
tricks in a circus, curves in a stream, these
        so called
simple pleasures – before commerce could
        pollute,
corrupt – before; does not every work of
        praise
remember and seek Eden?

Georges Seurat
inspired by small works in the collection
about 1883-1891
Musée d'Orsay, Paris

What a great moralist and painter he is – Toulouse-Lautrec

Le Lit

The two tired after all tender women in bed,
        for a while
not man handled, not handling money and the
        illusions aggressions
of men…but tired, but still capable
        of tenderness
understanding; by the relief of this sleep,
        by this
understanding women in weariness, saint
        Lautrec understands.

Henri de Toulouse-Lautrec
Le Lit
1892
Musée d'Orsay, Paris

Awake for the Massacre of the Innocents may be at Hand!

Ah, dear Vincent,
victor and Visionary, you
       must stir it all up,
fields of sunflowers or cypresses or olive trees
       or pictures of the
floating world from the Japanese or vain
       colorful Gauguin,
soil, soul; even these pine trees in the asylum
       garden become
phrases in the Burning Bush, become brothers
       to the pain that
is part of the glory of your search for God.

Vincent van Gogh
PINE TREES IN THE ASYLUM GARDEN
1889
Musée d'Orsay, Paris

Some night scenes by Whistler

Some night scenes by Whistler
     and I close my eyes,
open them, close them, how do owls whistle, what
     do they know?
avoiding the garish and harsh light by day and disaster,
     one introduces mist and distance
and the Whistler dreams of Japan, distance, softness, dusk;
     then there are the shadows
the peacock feathers make in the memory, the music and
     the transcendental peacock feathers
that come from that, the poet novelist leans her head
     towards death and music and Mrs. Ramsey.

James Abbot McNeill Whistler
Inspired by paintings of night scenes
dates unknown
as seen at the Musée d'Orsay, Paris

Mother calmly honored by a son –
best wishes from Whistler

She's sedentary, calm, proud
      of him,
Whistler's mother, as day after day
      he makes a
seated profile panorama subtle of her,
      she puts up
with his long time esthetic shenanigans,
      he's being
ecstatic again, this time with subtle tones of
      grey, etc.
A delicate lace cap crowns her; she knows
      that year
after year, painting after painting
      he has been
religious in devotion to light, his work,
      his subjects.

James Abbot McNeill Whistler
ARRANGEMENT IN GREY AND BLACK NO. 1:
PORTRAIT OF THE ARTIST'S MOTHER
1871
Musée d'Orsay, Paris

Great expanse, late afternoon, high view at the
top of the Musée d'Orsay..............more clouds now

How many views?
of Mt. Fuji? of Santa Maria del Fiore?
of the Seine from way up here on the terrace by the
      large stone statues
of distant Sacré-Coeur. We vaguely remember the 1st view
      from up magnificent
here; and could this be the last view? There in the distance
      is the fine high
white dome of Sacré-Coeur, not far from where we live,
      there it is
somewhat like a huge white egg shell. Vague sounds of
      an occasional
barge below, more frequent buses. Fragments of
      international
languages nearby; breeze; solitary inquisitive
      sparrow near
immense perched statues; I continue to scribble.
      The Seine
once seen by Ronsard, Balzac, Baudelaire and
      all those
Impressionists inside; for the moment I say
      Merci Beaucoup
      and Good-bye, Sacré-Coeur

WASHINGTON, D.C.:

The National Gallery of Art

*I was wondering hours ago as I was joining the
crowds abandoning ship, going down my steep long
escalator– what are they all thinking of after all
that intake of imagery, how profound has it been,
for them, for me, what will be the residue, will there
be some evident and maybe lasting effect? After all
the paintings, prayers, pilgrimages what will be the
results, what metamorphosis will occur? We go to these
images by Leonardo, Vermeer, Rembrandt with such
instinctive need. What will happen to a pebble after
years of water flowing over it from heaven...
we are all wet. Yes, it is raining.*

I call you, Calder, at length and
In good forms we are lighter

Calder

you call to me

so I am a mobile

and then 300 other mobiles

your designs are wafted by the breeze

your mind turns   making us lightly behold

pleasure   millions travel and lightly turn

you colorfully   in   their   minds

where is the mind

Thank you for flight again

Calder
huge East Wing Calder
calling to me, sure, I prefer you
    to jets and huge planes,
you are hugely calm at times, mobile
    that makes my motions
and Imagination huge, calm, grandiose,
    serene, decorative, delicate.

Alexander Calder
UNTITLED
1976
National Gallery of Art, East Building, Washington, D.C.

Paul Cézanne
THE ARTIST'S FATHER
1866
National Gallery of Art, Washington, D.C.

One never enters the same stream twice
       and
one never reads the same sentences in the
       same way
and now that I am looking again magnified
       at the
Cézanne Figure of the Artist's Father reading
       a French
newspaper I know that painting like poetry
       is news
which always remains news, is seen in
       new ways
every day we are alive.

How many decisions and constructions are Possible?

A deck of cards –
rich man, poor man, beggar man,
>> thief,
Chardin, Cézanne, calculator and chaos,
>> speculations,
losses, gains, landslides, my horse
>> won; I
collect the songs; there's architecture
>> built in to
the wings, the mind; fables of forms are
>> intricate;
the well-built theater has gamblers,
>> adventurers,
lawyers, designers, all the characters of Shakespeare,
>> O fragile
house of cards, of clowns, of saints, more or less
>> lovers; we pray
>> and play
>> for you.

Jean Siméon Chardin
THE HOUSE OF CARDS, *detail*
1735
National Gallery of Art, Washington, D.C.

Some leaves above him, mostly in shadow and to the side
a leisurely fellow
at a window sill is blowing soap bubbles,
    introspective
refined gentleman observed by a curious child;
    now and
then something enlarged a universe, this delicate
    large
bubble is very large, reflects some lights, the
    brow
of the gentleman with fine hair is enlightened,
    or is
he poor and passing the time?; we know we always know
    very little
about the Creator or Creation.

Jean Siméon Chardin
SOAP BUBBLES, *detail*
1745
National Gallery of Art, Washington, D.C.

After seeing many Balanchine Dances and
after seeing many Degas Scenes of Ballet Dancers

Gasps
of post-consummation,
gasps of fish caught, receding waves after we
      were overwhelmed,
I wondered why God wrote all this music
      for us to overhear.

Edgar Degas
THE DANCE LESSON
c. 1879
National Gallery of Art, Washington, D.C.

Matisse, you make me feel real cool,
     nothing is burning me,
nothing is irritating me or you, there isn't
     disintegration or preaching or
desiring or the oppression of yearning and nada,
     nothing is static and nothing
     is Faustian motion.
It is all noble, it is all innocence, it is all
     painting, satisfaction and perfection.
I certainly prefer it to Dante's Heaven.
It is exactly where I want to arrive.

Henri Matisse
inspired by the Matisse room with LA NÉGRESSE
LARGE COMPOSITION WITH MASKS,
WOMAN WITH AMPHORA AND POMEGRANATE, *and* VENUS
1952-53
National Gallery of Art, Washington, D.C.

The Rose Period; Two Adolescents

Arms upraised and resting on his head, naked, cool,
     still capable
of hearing as if from a sea shell some of the music
     he heard before he
and his mother were born; what is he dreaming of as
     he stands in the dawn?
before angst, before price and search and desire for
     possession; free of that
which makes for violence or confusion; he is present;
     she is present, cool naked
companion, jug on her head, back to us; both innocent, both
     part of the dawn.

Pablo Picasso
Two Adolescents
1906
National Gallery of Art, Washington, D.C.

View of Arles with Irises in the Foreground

A row of saints, a stream of irises, urgent co-operators
    with the urgent
growing earth, irises, Rimbaud illuminations hidden in the
    shadow ready
to escape into the poem of each touch, the paint brush with
    its wet
thickness touches and blesses Being in its variations of color,
    its vibrations of prayer.
After the ecstasies of these communions, the respected cities
    of man are put in perspective.
Respect. Work. Learn from the Irises of the Fields.

Vincent van Gogh
VIEW OF ARLES
1888
National Gallery of Art, Washington, D.C.

Johannes Vermeer
A WOMAN HOLDING A BALANCE
1664
National Gallery of Art, Washington, D.C.

A Woman Holding a Balance

There's light on her calmly curved brow,
        a glow,
just as there could be and would be on a
        pearl,
I know she is again calmly pregnant
        accepting
the glow wondering about the day the
        future and
what balance and care she can keep maintaining
        hope procedure
he studies her, caring adding art to light,
        their care
keeps the world in balance. To look into
        this room
for a moment steadies the soul.

Johannes Vermeer
A Lady Writing
1665
National Gallery of Art, Washington, D.C.

A Lady Writing

A lady writing pleased turns her head
    in pensiveness,
the choices she makes, the letters of the alphabet,
    love by letter,
directed by selectivity and the soul, the messages
    are received
by Johannes as he cares for every subtle detail of
    beauty, light
on the white fur, the varied blue that covers the
    writing table,
the tiny pearls, all, the light glow of her
    curved brow.

WASHINGTON, D. C.:

The Phillips Collection

Here and light blue….introspective Raoul Dufy
The Artist's Studio

Everybody
needs a nude
in an artist's studio
cool thigh   cool desire   buds
of nipples   supple coolness   feel here
be balmy   be a bee   sting me here
see me singing in the temple's inner ear

Raoul Dufy
THE ARTIST'S STUDIO
1935
Phillips Collection, Washington, D.C.

117

Henri Matisse
STUDIO, QUAI ST. MICHEL
1916
Phillips Collection, Washington, D. C.

118

Rainbows, vibrations, colors,
what are you leading us to?

What are we
wanting when we are
resting naked? It's more
than a Matisse painting of
a nude in his studio, it's
more than the 10 millionth
orgasm, though those and
Matisse's images are desirable,
it's more even than Quixote's
desire for Dulcinea; what is
it that keeps us afloat lofty
as sensible desirable myths in
Tiepolo? What did Adam and Eve
desire before so called rational
arguments commanded them?
Fruition said the fruit;
we have rented a room said
Matisse to the model, for the
time being we must imagine
each other, satisfaction, desire,
restlessness as best we can.

Joan Miró
THE RED SUN
1948
Phillips Collection, Washington, D.C.

120

Composer or the Red Sun

What's the use anyway
Juan Miró   how many
years have I admired you
Juan Miró why though is
it so I know why it is
so Juan Miró   of course
you know me Juan Miró
sure you admire me Juan
Miró you do all sorts of
fantasies to us   Juan Miró
I suppose so   I suppose so and
now you know we have something
more or less to show for the
music that has been proposing
us all these years signed by
the Spaniard who conquered comedy.

Small Bonnard painting of a woman on a horse

The circus rider
on Pegasus was
giving Apollinaire
and e.e. cummings
and Seurat and others
the go around.

Pierre Bonnard
Circus Rider
1936-1946
Phillips Collection, Washington, D. C.

Snow in April

We in Maine know what
that's like and in May too,
you will see it melt, a
snowman too, nourishing the
ground for summer and autumn
leaves, we were aghast at first,
but at last colorful delighted
we saw the daintiness celebration
of Maurice Prendergast

Maurice Prendergast
Snow in April
1907
Phillips Collection, Washington, D.C.

NEW YORK:

The Metropolitan Museum of Art

*It is my planned way to be resourceful, to take what I
can from paintings and from cities as I go, to steal the
lute, to enter a color; not of course to be an historian,
art or otherwise, with other pretensions. Out comes
the blue notebook and the moveable séance begins.*

PABLO PICASSO
PORTRAIT OF GERTRUDE STEIN
1906
Metropolitan Museum of Art, New York

124

Portrait of Gertrude Stein

Bulk, Sphinx,
Jewish, American, know-it-all,
        Stone, Stein, Gertrude,
Pyramid, Am I; when this you see
        remember me; am
here to hear, to make the Making
        of Americans,
established with Alice in Wonderland and at
        Rue de Fleurus;
address me correctly in the universe; riddles and
        aphorisms and phrases;
Tender Buttons; nouns. Plays. Once I am sufficient
        you are Sufi, you
        are busy.

At Columbus and Broadway

It's an El of a Ride in Brooklyn and the Queens and
                    Manhattan,
flimsy and noisy above ground thousands rattle
                    along to
work and entertainment, above ground, below ground,
                    near and far,
in fear and laughter, desiring and weariness,
                    absorbing
more or less thousands of images and sensations,
                    arriving
at an exit turnstile, ending an El of a day.

Berenice Abbott
EL AT COLUMBUS AVENUE AND BROADWAY
1929
Metropolitan Museum of Art, New York

Near Grand Central Station

Luncheon Window, NYC,
3 tired office workers facing out to NYC streets
and endless
passersby, the somewhat stymied office workers
chewing and
chewing away at their sandwiches, give us this
day our
daily drudgery, and then all sorts of billions of
more or
less tired workers all over the world at different
times of day
munching on their food as they try to digest the past
and
wonder what next? what next in the future?

Unknown Photographer
Near Grand Central Station
date unknown
Metropolitan Museum of Art, New York

Bacchante by the Sea

There is a Corot harmony dewiness coolness
      between
the calm beauty of the extended nude
      woman
in repose and the dark green between her
      and me
and the dark green undulations hills bushes
      behind her
relaxed pleased body. Slight sleep, sensual
      drowsiness,
she rests partly on a leopard skin, in the
      bluish distance
a small pool; we are bright very close to
      satisfaction, sleep,
we sense dew by the moss, you want to
      be there too.

Jean-Baptiste Camille Corot
BACCHANTE BY THE SEA
1865
Metropolitan Museum of Art, New York

128

Wanting to make good Impressions

Hats, just democratic crowns, practical,
      playful,
a display of flowery bonnets by Degas and
      the pretty woman milliner
makes us smile. Imagine on the boulevard of
      your fantasy the
young woman who will wander into the Millinery
      Shop and see what decor
adorns her beauty best. Imagine us, lovers of
      beauty and paintings, the
millionaires of pleasure wandering through the Tuileries
      toward joyous designs and
      colors in museums.

Edgar Degas
The Millinery Shop *and* At the Milliner's
1882-1886
Metropolitan Museum of Art, New York

The Repast of the Lion

Businessman at the club luncheon;
like a somewhat tired and slightly guilty financier
          after a committee meeting
eating his thick sirloin steak, the little Henri Rousseau
          lion in the high
thick wide jungle leaves with his bloody mouth eats his
          spotted little leopard-like
victim; is it a vicious cycle? eating and being eaten; the
          white sun rises and sets;
the heavy exotic plants droop; a few wide flowers in the
          still wide masticating
air open; momentary mortuary stillness after the
          stock market has closed. A finish
          to exotic financiers.

Henri Rousseau
THE REPAST OF THE LION
1907
Metropolitan Museum of Art, New York

Portraits of Georgia O'Keeffe

The aging face   the aging hands   the
  aging body
ah so so   it must be   like waterfalls
  time passes
the body   breast   changes   where there is
  motion and emotion
and the sight of light and dark and the transformation
  of the galaxy
by the flea or you or me   there is time   so it must be
  the aging face
the aging hands   all the changing mysteries
  and beauty
lines under the eyes   don't be monotonous with
  sighs about this
be like the changing skies   rain   reign
  with laughter be
  like the ancient
  taoists

Alfred Stieglitz
inspired by photographs of Georgia O'Keeffe
1917-1931
Metropolitan Museum of Art, New York

PROVIDENCE, RHODE ISLAND:

Museum of Art
Rhode Island School of Design

I like paintings and poems that help me
love the world more, sea, clouds, people,
pebbles, and so forth, irises, sunflowers…

Rain on the River

Noisy willful
iron industry and manmade train
puffing and roaring away by the heavy calm
    or turbulent
Hudson River by millions of moving New Yorkers
    in Riverside Park or on
Big City streets; breathing, puffing away, smoking
    away, talking fast or
slow; a modern grand concert of motions.

George Bellows
RAIN ON THE RIVER
1908
RISD Museum, Providence

George Braque
Still Life
1918
RISD Museum, Providence

Still Life

I just want to be quiet, my
    painting and I,
I just want to construct, Stillness,
    a life, my
steadiness and attention; I am abstracted
    into thought,
my own music of cubism, I listen to
    one tone talk
to another, one color talk to another, what
    you might call
a grape talking to another grape. Grapple
    with metaphysics
and me.

Paul Cézanne
Banks of a River
1900-06
RISD Museum, Providence

136

The sound of order in color

Banks of a river by Cézanne, that's where
          to deposit
your valuables and increase your interests
          securely
and in a way that will benefit your health,
          the color
in your contemplation; the control of fluency of
          a river
or inspiration or breathing or contemplation, that
          makes for
munificence. In plein air become a millionaire
          of freshness.
Let it go at that. Nonpossessive love will make
          you the
richest in possessions. When something is so precious
          and priceless
you cannot lose your wealth. Those Cézanne
          Clouds are
looking down on us; he knew what to hope for, rivers
          will resound.

Thomas Cole
GENESEE SCENERY
1847
RISD Museum, Providence

Genesee Scenery

Secluded sounding generous
        active
waterfall, why did I seek you out?
        I admiring you,
flow of vitality from the sky, from the
        earth,
consciousness resounding, inevitable
        urgency,
power of beauty, power of fluency, voice,
        every second
new (in some divine woodland), wet fluent
        vocabulary,
religious relative to clouds and streams,
        moving
vigorous dancer over rocks, your
        indescribable
ancestors are active in your voice, your
        wet connotations,
pounding, sounding, upsurging, you're
        giving painters
something to wet their brushes for. You are
        continuing our old
        new celebration.

Winslow Homer
ON A LEE SHORE
1900
RISD Museum, Providence

On a Lee Shore

You've heard and you've seen stupendous heavy ascending
        and assaulting
surging climbing bursting very heavy waves in creation
        motion and
wonder if Zeus and/or Neptune might feel inferior to that,
        those splendid
mythological show offs. Winslow Homer in depicting this
        was slowly
exultant calmly composing; So? So there are proceeding
        waves of wonder.

Édouard Manet
REPOSE
1870-71
RISD Museum, Providence

142

You too
change as I change,
suggestions pour from your radiance,
person I love, or painting I see, as light on
        a stream does;
signs of vitality are sacred, my faith and
        imagination say,
so this beautiful pensive young Manet woman
        in repose
on her divan has a flowing light of white on
        her rich dress
which Manet divined, gave reflective glory to
        as she rested
and was gentle brilliant for the rest of
        our lives.

Repose can be receptive to what is glowing

Claude Monet
The Seine at Giverny
1895
RISD Museum, Providence

So care increases our fluency and strength

Have I taken care of you, "Seine at
        Giverny"?
have I been sane enough? saved enough? cool
        enough, fresh
enough, to reflect with the clouds and the
        thoughts of Monet?
coolness and sanity of pleasure and reflection is
        what I want.
I've been to Giverny several times. To regard
        a painting
in a continuing stream of consciousness way is
        clearly a
reason for part of my love of life ways.

Prairie in Eragny

Cloudy weather and careful munching
      slow moving
cows in dew, slow motion and you
      we hope in
coolness and meditation; this is
      Pissarro's
meditation (1888) *Prairie in Eragny,*
      radiant light
light tiny green points glowingly
      together,
that makes for soft green Peace; now
      worried we
in August 2002 pray and wish to work
      for Peace;
we need the slow motion, music, of people
      in communion,
calm French vacation pleasures, the milk of
      human kindness.
Maternal carefulness. Some wetness. Mild cloudy.
      Glowing blessings.

Camille Pissarro
PRAIRIE À ERAGNY
1888
Seen at an exhibit at RISD Museum, Providence

146

Caught up by the illustrious painter of pleasure
and his subject

And we get caught up in her rich soft sort of
          orange gold hair
and get attracted by the salmon pink armchair
          she is sitting in
her back mostly to us and we get caught up
          by the soft
sort of blue wool sweater she is wearing and
          by the pink of
her cheek and the slightest view of her lips,
          easily we are
caught up by the warm tints, texture, tones, colors,
          music of the painting.

Pierre-Auguste Renoir
YOUNG WOMAN READING AN ILLUSTRATED JOURNAL
1880
RISD Museum, Providence

Theodore Robinson
AFTERNOON SHADOWS
1891
RISD Museum, Providence

A view with you in mind

Theodore Robinson (1852-96)
In 1891 before his early death painted for us
        "Afternoon Shadows";
so much green so much light delicate lyrical
        green in this
scene long after (today August 26, 2001) the season
        and reasons of
his affection changed; we continue to change for the
        better as we
view this field of delicate green and a little mound
        like a
pantheistic transcendental shrine of hay is seen.
        I believe
a poem or painting has a way of seeing and
        saving us.

Henri Rousseau
FLOWERS IN A VASE
1909-1910
RISD Museum, Providence

Flowers in a Vase

To be intent
and perfectly prepared to respect
      and
respond with one's unique subjectivity and skill
      to a
vase of flowers a year or two before one's
      death
is a sign of purity, joy, and progress,
      a gesture
of happiness and generosity – also for us later
      seers passing
the time admiring this sign of his eternity.

A Corner of a Park at Belleview, Autumn Sunset

Now I am in a corner
and I am calm and intimate with you,
　　　Henri Rousseau painting,
(there is a sort of light vague lavender sunset),
　　　I notice every
single small leaf you made, Henri, what
　　　surprise, patience,
order and delight, the trees and branches narrow,
　　　so much sky
is seen. There is a narrow central path, a
　　　well-disciplined
quaint guard, upstanding, bemused; I think
　　　you liked everything
you touched; so I find it all intimate; it is
　　　a quiet cozy
autumn; in a touched way all concerned are pleased.

Henri Rousseau
A CORNER OF A PARK AT BELLEVIEW
Autumn Sunset
1902
RISD Museum, Providence

Boating Party near Calcot Mill, Reading

Singer can vacation and
sing in his pleased and amazing and consoling and
      splendor making
lyrical painting caring and careful way; composition;
      meditation;
patience and gentleness and appreciation and artistic
      skill can
help; this Sargent leads us to sing, helps
      give meanings
      to vacations.

John Singer Sargent
BOATING PARTY NEAR CALCOT MILL, READING
1889
RISD Museum, Providence

John Singer Sargent
PORTRAIT OF THE ARTIST SKETCHING
1922
RISD Museum, Providence

A feeling of connection

Twigs, forest, stone, nearby
        slightly seen
sea, you are subjects worth drawing,
        I wish I
could do you too, unseen visitor in
        the future
to my canvas, I have an endless
        curiosity and
respect, want to reflect, capture,
        via my
brush strokes; I'm all alone (1922)
        painting. That
happened the year before I, the scribbler
        in Providence (1999)
was born in Italy (1923). Later in 1953
        my wife and I
lovers of Italy, Maine, and Sargent,
        went to Maine.
To me this seems like a Maine place
        we often visited.
In a certain sense, Singer Sargent,
        your and my poems
are timeless – or so we feel.

Eugene Vail
The Grand Canal, Venice
ca. 1904
RISD Museum, Providence

Hoping you reflect about this and more
in moving appreciative ways

Reflections concerning reflections concerning reflections
and more reflections
as tiny waves of reflected sun in the Venice Grand Canal
Scene by Impressionist
Influenced reflective lyrical Eugene Vail (ca. 1904);
I was reflecting there
recently a few months ago (yr. 2001) and for the
first time in Autumn
1952; I now in the autumn of my life, long time
educated by the
reflections of many French Impressionists. Debussy
and we know that
notes of music like ripples in the Grand Canal change
and change; we change
but Keats' poems and this know a thing of beauty
is a joy forever.

Vincent van Gogh
VIEW OF ARLES
1888
RISD Museum, Providence

View of Arles

After all everything alive, you, me, and
        in art
is palpitating, giving itself eternally away,
        vibrant
in van Gogh and others, no soul's expression
        is lost,
no brushstroke is not as alive as a
        rabbit
or rapid or still angel. This field of
        weeds, reeds,
few flowers, few trees, with Arles in
        the distance
and awe and palpitations in the seer,
        is as rich
momentous as all life must be. It
        and we
celebrate the generosity of van Gogh in Arles
        and here
in Providence; I agree, it's ecstasy,
        it is
sound; all art and soulful life is
        music.

III   Poems Inspired by Favorite Artists

*In Italy where I was when I was a child and ever
since then I've been drawn to the pleasure of looking
at pictures; there before I was 7 I would gape at the
pictures of saints in churches and in market places.
And we've gone all over the world looking for them
(the saints?) the pictures.*

Fra Angelico
SAINT MICHAEL
1424
Private Collection
Seen at a special exhibition, Musée du Luxembourg, Paris, 2000

Saint Michael

SAINT MICHAEL – upstanding winged youth,
all in blue, his wings and tunic spotted with
          gold;
victorious he overcame the dragon demon, easily
          he stands
flattening him out with the weight of faithful
          capability,
that strength of goodness, if Michael so desired,
          could uplift
with heavenly lightness. This Fra Angelico quality
          is here
depicted with quiet Fra Angelico strength.

Winter Landscape with Skaters

Gliding gliding warming up gliding gliding, keeping one's
          hands in one's
mittens, keeping one's thoughts on the girlfriend or angels of
          snowflakes, or if
old and bold enough on God…gliding gliding on canals frozen over,
          on experiences
from the past that lead us to pleasure-and-exhaustion,
          sex, religion or
hot chocolate, all this varies according to the skater or
          lover. Now put on
your skates, go from Dutch winter painting to Dutch
          winter painting or
from one of my winter or many Maine poems and glide glide
          with praises for
the winter and sky and the makers of skates, poems and
          pleasures. And
sometimes with holiday company glide glide…

Hendrick Avercamp
Winter Landscape with Skaters
1608
Rijksmuseum, Amsterdam

The effectiveness of generosity mirrored

Basket of fruit
reflected in a mirror, 1946
reflected in the imagination
of the gentle and colorful
philosopher who is reflecting
concerning a poem that
is reflecting concerning
the goodness of Bonnard (1986).

Pierre Bonnard
BASKET OF FRUIT
1946
Seen at a special exhibition, Musée Maillol, Paris, 2000

165

Nu Orange

The growing lost
nude near and
is her found
all above in
orange her the
and and fragrance
fragrant we
like who
the are
many
many
oranges
that
are

Pierre Bonnard
NU ORANGE
1940
Seen at a special exhibition, Musée Maillol, Paris, 2000

NOTES:

Bonnard – not photo realism but particular soul's lyricism, an intimate personal way of freedom, communion, praising light, fruit, flower, tablecloth, leaves, wetness, the body of a woman coming out of a bath, focusing on the flourishing and poetry of all that. Warm colors, not grey and black, not the linear which defines, but a kind of impressionism which reveals the glow of objects, the radiance of the soul. How good, how beneficial, how Bonnard to find such subjectivity-colors. The choice of colors reveals the painter's genetic makeup, whether it amounts to Braque or Delacroix or Bonnard, etc. What a kaleidoscope the expression of a free individual makes – and what a kaleidoscope the expression of all personalities in the world makes! Monstrous how some dictators and cultures have tried more or less to standardize everything, how some have tried to group people into one death camp of fascist brown or nazi black or Chairman Mao uniforms, uniformity. Pleasing need not mean superficial slight or frivolous though to some modern judges it seems to mean that. Maillol is pleasing too; thank the Mediterranean gods.

Still Life with Oysters

Preciously close to me, intimately appreciated,
        these subdued reflections,
those open oyster shells, that patient full lemon
        waiting to be squeezed
that almost disguised slender glass with white wine,
        that folded complication
of a white cloth (test for a painter's skill) here a
        luminous sensuous
success; and to one side slightly hidden - is it some
        kind of panettone?
and to my left, on that dark brown table, tall above the
        rest in semi-darkness
a glass water pitcher with various shades of grey and
        white; both near and far
Boudin sees it all composed carefully, Apollonian,
        and contemplates, composes,
sees it all from a very great distance.
        Calm. A triumph.

Eugène Boudin
STILL LIFE WITH OYSTERS
1850
Bristol Museum and Art Gallery, UK

A Venetian dim dark blue sky with two tiny clouds

Canaletto
by a canal with a canvas with a candor of
      pleasure and
quiet tones of music educated by Venice is
      again
learning from the façades of San Marco and the
      Doge's Palace
and from a subdued glow of light from those
      opulent
harmonious places. A few people, and fewer cats in
      the Piazza.
Music became architecture and educated the harmonies
      of Canaletto.

Canaletto
PIAZZA SAN MARCO
1740
Seen at a special exhibition, in the Musée du Luxembourg, Paris, 2000

The Clarifications of the Master

A glass of water, a few apples, a lemon,
      Cézanne
comes in and steadies the soul. Certain
      tones too
construct, organize; for me this is higher
      mathematics,
highest music. The different shades of blue, my
      different desires
for you led me to this victory or mountain
      continuing vibrations
      of still life.

Paul Cézanne
THE PEPPERMINT BOTTLE
1893/1895
National Gallery of Art, Washington D.C.

"Le Rocher Rouge" or the Order of the Day

Boulder, who can be
bolder than Cézanne, soft trees, green tones,
        side cliff
boulder, various shades of tan, pyramids are not
        bolder, more
mathematical. Nothing is flat or bland, here's
        inner dialogue
and a subtle varied clear sky. Contemplation is the
        order of the day.

Paul Cézanne
LE ROCHER ROUGE
1897
Musée de l'Orangerie, Paris

Dans le Parc du Château-Noir

Cézanne, so strong,
so determined, considering how you give
respect, those careful delicate tones, consideration
by consideration, subtle; respect this impulse, what
is the pulse the heart beating for if not to make this
        scene we see;
recreation cooperates with Creation carefully even musically in
        a human way.

Paul Cézanne
DANS LE PARC DU CHÂTEAU-NOIR
1900
Musée de l'Orangerie, Paris

Construction is Meditation

I reckoned
I was not a complete wreck yet,
        just give me time,
reminded myself as I wandered
        glowingly through
the museums that Turner would turn my way
        and allow
his sunsets and battleships to flare ignited by me,
        I figured
that my desireful work could still help
        plants grow,
summer come. Images like fruit arranged
        became
symphonies and mountains, one Sainte-Victoire,
        for me
and Cézanne. Though much in the world is
        often
tarnished and falling, aged strong Cézanne is
        constructive.

Pommes et biscuits

Some people can
administer angels but here it's
     Cézanne with
apples and a few biscuits. If those are
     apples what is
purest music? when love becomes precise
     colorful we can
call it Cézanne still life.

Cézanne said that with an apple he wanted to astonish Paris.

A still life can instill life in Cézanne and me.

Paul Cézanne
POMMES ET BISCUITS
1880
Musée de l'Orangerie, Paris

The Tall Trees at the Jas de Bouffan

Somebody said Cézanne and the tall trees sprang from
        the earth
it was coolest Spring, lightest variations of clarity, charity
        of lightest
varied shades of green, very natural for the genius, very
        vibrant for
the Necessity presenting depicting Cézanne-and-scene.
        Space unpolluted,
amid cool sky; this is where Adam walked and
        dreamt of God.

Paul Cézanne
TALL TREES AT THE JAS DE BOUFFAN
1885
Courtauld Gallery, London

The precision of reverence is tactful, heard and visible

The sublimity of the moving light in a gem
    treasures the mind and
the sublimities of every second of this music by Cézanne,
    different shades of mostly blue,
    some green water,
mountains, trees, known and imagined mountains, secluded
    place of creation where we
    are recreated;
refreshed by Cézanne someone almost fainted;
    Rilke revived.

Paul Cézanne
LAC D'ANNECY
1896
Courtauld Gallery, London

Wait for me later on

I am not up to you today,
    Cézanne,
I keep looking in the direction of your
    cool green
painting, what do I want from it? revival?
    reconstruction?
today that I do not seem able to co-create,
    to receive a
stimulus from it. My memory knows for sure
    your magnificence,
your rage for order, your coming to an epiphany
    of calmness, greenness,
coolness in southern France, the delicate early Springtime
    leaves coming to some
tree. You know what treasure to measure. Your
    work of contemplation,
though I am somewhat dormant at this moment
    you arouse my hope for
    future recreation.

A Young Student at his desk or Melancholy

Why melancholy adolescence? ask Keats, ask
         some grandchildren of mine,
why? why such perplexity and insecurity and
         deep sadness entering
upon maturity, aware of what? a lonely
         young man
in greys and tans leans heavily upon his desk,
         what has he
already learned? later also ask the melancholy
         notes of
Chopin; what dream in the womb has been
         given up
that makes one so weary (and hopeless?)
         before the
secular and merchant business begins?

Pieter Codde
A Young Scholar in the Study
1630-1633
Musée des Beaux-Arts, Lille, France

*It does help make one love humanity to see that one can see the way
Corot sees. Restores faith in the sanctity of the heart.*

Camille Corot

> I caught you,
> I caught you at it,
> the brush stroke, the soul-mood,
> the calm idyllic lyric way you saw a calm brook,
> > a young woman
> in the woods, light, shade, Springtime, every time
> > I return to
> You it's a vita nuova. Your reverence for light
> > captures us
> > lightly.

Resource

> Why is that eccentric tree so memorable? Bent
> > and somewhat isolated
> but Corot found it crowned it with his
> > memorable light,
> the enlightenment of the known as the light on wet
> > leaves after the rain
> delicately depicted creates a space of quietness where
> > the wishes of Wordsworth become true.

Le Lac, effet de nuit

> Full dim round moon over a lake, two
> > wandering
> on its reflection in the very slightly moving lake,
> > one the painter,
> one the reader, at once the mystery is everywhere.

Three poems inspired by painatings of Corot

Les Sources de la Loue

Grottoes you know,
you don't know, sources all your
          resources
can't altogether know. Awesome you know.
          Semblances
of scenes, of dreams, you show. Mystified
          respectful
          you go.

Gustave Courbet
LES SOURCES DE LA LOUE
1863
Zurich, Kuntshaus

Courbet's lavish sensual "La Bacchante en repos"

The wine spills   voluptuosness   rhythm
          sleep
her luscious nude body slightly turns
          curves
her rich fine breasts had been pleased   had
          pleased
had startled the world again   the color of the
          curved rich
body and its shadows, largesse of a caress,
          satisfaction
to swooning and sleep for lover, reader, seer
          and adored one.

Gustave Courbet
LA BACCHANTE EN REPOS
1844-47
Private Collection

Some bed sheets and some works of art
(this pastel scene for instance) give
rise to Occasions for Praise

An 1818 unmade bed still unmade –
　　how much
pitching and tossing, how much pushing and shoving,
　　so called
"love making," how much frustration, desire, how many dreams
　　and plans
for new works he urgently had God knows, what we comfortably
　　know is that
he made of this disturbed mountain of many bedsheets a
　　work of art
and for 35 more years made very well some with much
　　complex color
and commotion many grand Romantic paintings. While
　　seeing them
I lived more dramatically and later slept better.

Eugène Delacroix
Untitled Pastel Drawing
1818
Musée Delacroix, Paris

181

Carel Fabritius
THE GOLDFINCH
1654
Mauritshuis, The Hague

The Goldfinch

A balanced use of color in your life? (but are
        you a painter and
is life a canvas?), such balance could improve your
        moderation and
therefore your intensity; organization is necessary for a
        painting's power
(but are you an artist, is life a composition?); look
        how the
goldfinch is sedate, seems sedentary, gaining power to perhaps
        inspire our
philosophic flight. Who is the goldfinch now?

Giovanni di Paolo
THE CREATION
1445
Metropolitan Museum of Art, New York
Seen at Pinacoteca, Siena

The Creation

To set one of the worlds Spinning, to
    set one of the
Words spinning, to fire up the ecstasies,
    to start a
Child spelling a bible, learning to subscribe
    to sending
love; circles of consciousness kept turning and
    turning in the
widening gyre; gymnastics of angels contributed
    strength for
saints; painters became colorful; Siena appeared
    with memories of the
    City of God on a hill.

Annette the startled mind-reader
(imagined by Giacometti)

distant
relative
of
Giacometti
why
are
you
always
dimly
but
intensely
staring
from
your
window
your
present
prison
of
this
life?

Three poems inspired by works of Alberto Giacometti

Self-Conscious among the Lost

Though
I saw the
Giacometti tall tall tall lonely man
many many many years ago he didn't stop growing
the sun of the author helped by your view of things
made his shadow flicker at length,
it was what Plato said
in one of his myths

Sundial as Quixote

the
long
thin
growing
extended
shadow
of
the
tall
tall
thin
Giacometti
figure
indicates
a
long
history
of
isolation

Her name is Vairaumati

Baffled Gauguin, what can he bank on? what
         gold?
not here, not there, but somewhere; pursuing
         persisting
baffled Gauguin, I ask for a sacred object to
         bow to,
I only partly capable of prayer, wanting to go as
         far as
prayer can take one, beyond Tahiti, beyond
         this any place,
to begin to read the map of the gold of the
         soul of the body.

Paul Gauguin
Her name is Vairaumati
1892
Pushkin Museum, Moscow

La Carità
seems pregnant

> and sedentary, calm, fulfilled, related to
> Toscana, Umbria, olive orchards
> and don't forget Giotto; he
> didn't forget

the pregnant world and God, Aquinas, Agriculture and Mother,

> forms enlarged
> by Sun and Music
> and Love;

more work led to large Churches, Madonnas in

> Mystery; bambini;

charity seems to hold some worldly goods in her generous calm,
warmth; a gourd, a curving cornucopia that seems to go out of
bounds;

> the ground is blessed;

the ground work of our faith will be like your next poem.

Giotto
LA CARITÀ (CHARITY) SCULPTURE
Thirteenth Century
Museum of the Cathedral, Florence

La Scultura (Sculpture)

Someone like Giotto
Artist and Artisan, not flimsy or falling,
is forming   is forming   is Making a Poem

La Pittura (Painting)

No one is sturdier more passionate more attentive
than this remarkable painter dreaming up order
designing it boldly with strong necessity making his mark.
concentration and color, space and form – celebration to be noted!

L'Architettura (Architecture)

Sitting
Substantial
Constructive
Mathematical
precise pensive attentive keeping at it
dreaming up houses, dreaming up churches and all that goes with them
making symbols of heaven to live in, to pray in.

*Three poems suggested by scenes in bas relief plaques which decorate the
Bell Tower for the Cathedral of Florence by Giotto (there are more
than 20, some by Giotto, some by Andrea Pisano and assistants).*

NOTES

*Almost 50 years ago I first saw, was touched in the head forever,
by the scenes of Giotto in Assisi. And here I am Reminded.
Re-mind, to find the mind again, to mine what is most
memorable, valuable. This great Giotto scene was made
according to Vasari for the Cathedral of Pisa which I visited
often (1950–52 and later). The golden messages from the
wounds of the feet of Christ and the wounds in the palms of
Christ pierce the hands and feet of the astounded reverent
Brother Francis. Small scenes below the large gold Stigmata
Scene with its few Umbrian trees depict St. Francis holding
up a tipsy church and St. Francis feeding and conversing with
a flock of birds. Birds of a feather flock together. The Winged
Christ of course has large feathers. There is a sense of intimacy
and privacy in these 2 dark and golden Giotto scenes. And the
huge Cimabue Majesty Scene, nothing gaudy, not the world
(beautiful as it can be of nature which can decay and be bombed)
but the Realm of the Human Heart and Hope which we have
to call Supernatural. As Emily from Amherst said, acquainted
with miracles, the supernatural is only the natural disclosed.*

The Young Flute Player

The dreamy attendant boy flute player with the
      dark red beret
is at ease playing his growing tune, violin and
      recorder hang on
the wall near his side. The colors of the artist
      keep us in an
auditorium of mildness, shadows, subtlety, listening,
      privacy and contemplation.

Judith Leyster
BOY PLAYING A FLUTE
1630-1635
National Museum, Stockholm

What can we do but
give ourselves away, the asparagus were doing that
       and Manet
elated delicate appreciative was waxing eloquent
       about them;
a strength in this kind, his and their, of delicacy
       helps us
in some sort of civilization survive. Which has its
       earthiness
and iridescence. Now to depict a bunch of
       asparagus as
Édouard Manet did is fine responsiveness. Respect
       and fine
responsiveness and freshness arouse genuine ineffable unique
       religions.
Handled with care by Manet or Proust or the graceful
       housewife
strength in part of civilization is maintained.

Édouard Manet
STILL LIFE WITH ASPARAGUS
1880
Wallraf-Richartz Museum, Cologne

Édouard Manet
THE BAR AT THE FOLIES-BERGÈRE
1881-82
Courtauld Gallery, London

A Bar at the Folies-Bergère

Liqueurs, champagne bottles gold topped ready to pop,
        huge glistening glass chandelier
reflected in a mirror, tangerines in the wide glass chalice,
        talkative French crowds in the café,
central icon of the bar maid somewhat perplexed tired
        confronting us and the inquisitive
propositioner in the top hat; failure at the Folies; folly
        and more gleaming bottles, laughter,
chit-chat and smoke; she calmly looms large, presented,
        patient, gift outright of service
and yet her thoughts birth hope original soul somewhere elsewhere,
        look, amidst the moons
all in our reflections, large communal mirror, the dismayed
        calm offered heroine, lips, bosom,
        graceful figure, evasive Eve
        is Central; Bergère; dim
        pink roses in a lucent
        glass; chalice.

La Jeune Fille et le Vase de Fleurs

Ah, Midi, ah, mild Provence afternoons, the balminess
        caressing,
the nude body of the jeune fille waking or walking in the
        summer afternoon
after the bath; walking naked as in a dream on the rose rug
        and by the white flowers,
part of a palm tree of Midi seen from the window; mildness;
        a green pillow; Matisse
perhaps in Venice or Nice or at least half asleep half awake
        adventuring. Humanists of the
world, unite, you have nothing to lose but your clothes.

Henri Matisse
La Jeune Fille et le Vase de Fleurs
1920
Musée de l'Orangerie, Paris

The Serf

Vulnerable bald old bearded fellow,
            nude with
a bit of a pot belly, his little old
            treasure sack
of testicles, still somewhat dreaming and
            erotic, a little
sturdy and shaken; once upon a time
            a bit of Pan,
still taking some dramatic stance and somewhat
            assertingly aged.

Henri Matisse
The Serf, *Bronze Sculpture*
1903
San Francisco Museum of Modern Art

The Marvelous Repose arrived at

Odalisque
in chair
nude and imagined
by Matisse and
by my need after
a grey day and a
million museums
in London
cool Mediterranean
Odalisque and Praise
ode

Henri Matisse
Odalisque
date unknown
Tate Gallery, London

Matisse's late Collages are
my College at Any Age

Matisse in Old Age, young wisdom, in the
kindergarten of
Beauty, a child at play by the
eternal sea.

Henri Matisse
Collages
dates unknown
Centre Pompidou, Paris

Who are the captains? Who are the captives?

Where have they come from? the UK, the USA, Germany,
        France, Spain,
Austria, Australia, everywhere in Europe, Japan, everywhere
        in Asia, everywhere
in North and South America, herded many in noisy groups,
        the tour guides
speaking in many languages, what are they emerging from?
        what are they
seeking amidst this noise? Michelangelo's strength art?
        one needs it
to survive; we are amidst the gigantic struggle, his
        captives forever
struggle to emerge from the rock to come once more
        into being.
Who is free? minding what the great mystery of the
        mind is
commanding. Michelangelo's faithfully determined soul
        strong still
struggling; the tensions of the body, the weight of
        the earth;
the commandments of the heart and mind, focused on the
        work; and so
day after day some part of the changing creation evolves.
        What drives
the hammer? John Donne, can you help answer? Blake,
        can you
help answer? Adam's consciousness startled started
        by the sun;
question answer; then make your prophetic remark, burning
        sacred Host.

Michelangelo
THE CAPTIVES, *Marble Sculpture*
1520-1530
Accademia Museum, Florence

199

Michelangelo
THE CREATION OF ADAM
1481-1482
Sistine Chapel Ceiling, Vatican, Rome

What was, what is, in the Future?!

O that well-made
handsome Italian nude slouch
waiting for the Patriarchal finger to charge him,
reclining well-made Adam into upright Active-David,
Biblical fellows of the Mighty sort; God knew what was
about to Come, the history from their loins, the
calms, the civilizations and cataclysms from
their complex Human Minds ! Adam in his
grand Reclining state oddly needed to
get into trouble, time, to have some
catastrophic tests, to give birth to
Cain and Abel, kings and beggars,
murderers, saints; he couldn't
just continue to recline, he,
we needed turbulence,
Michelangelo, etc.,
Jesus.

Michelangelo
BACCHUS
1497
Bargello Museum, Florence

Carved and curved for a truth which is beauty

And so
        Bacchus
to touch the curves of the body, to open the mouth, in
        a trance
to dance the sensual ever new sensual dance, delicious delight,
        pressing the
grapes, eyes closed; sensible youth, dreaming having learned
        from streams
having learned from the motions of plants and planets the
        need to savor,
the need to sleep and dance at the same time, young god of
        the grapes and goats,
of the vine and divine, young god whose play is prayer for
        rhythms, reverence
of the curve of the grape; we gaze we gape upon the slope
        of drowsing,
becoming sensible to the motions that lead the goat to feed.

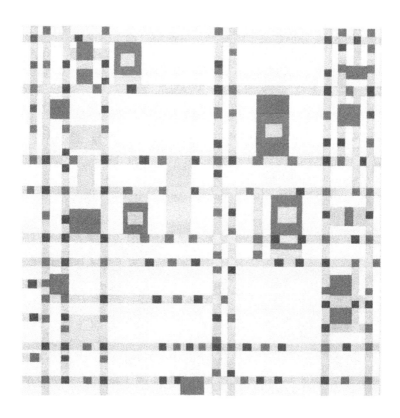

Piet Mondrian
BROADWAY BOOGIE-WOOGIE
1942-43
Mondrian Room, Museum of Modern Art, New York
© 2013 Mondrian/Holtzman Trust c/o HCR International USA

In a Mondrian Room of the Museum of Modern Art, N.Y.

Beads	views	notations
in	we	by
a	want	all
rosary	to	the
	have	composers
squares		
in	marks	ancestors
Mondrian	we	
	want	past and
windows	to	future
in	make	repeating
buildings		the rosaries

NOTES ON CLAUDE MONET

*Obviously Monet gave his time, his life, to his praise, his painting; and
So have I, though I am no judge of my self, I have come, I am here, and
Poems have come to me like the leaves to the trees.*

*Candle light in churches
with stained glass windows.
Color and lyrics of water
lilies surrounded by subdued
different tones of green and
blue; skies and water are
reflecting each other; lyrical
brush strokes are getting me
involved. I feel that if we leave
the earth and trees, flowers
the light and glory of nature
and seasons too completely, if
we become too abstracted from
this, from what suggested
our ideas, images, responses,
we become undernourished,
we lose strength, richness of
associations; Debussy and
Monet, Whitman and Van Gogh, my art teachers. I feel it's as if Monet
after looking and looking, absorbing and absorbing, closed his eyes,
slept the music of the colors into being. Looking at an object is actively
subjective, creative; being conversant with sleep and transformations
make Rilke and Monet objective in a strong meaningful human way.
There is no Aristotelian tragedy here, no beginning, middle, or end; a
changing moment or eternity is caught in its palpitating way by the
painter who opens his eyes and paints.*

Claude Monet
ROUEN CATHEDRAL, WEST FAÇADE
1894
National Gallery of Art, Washington, D. C.

Freshness is all

To have a sense of breeze in a painting,
a sense of the playfulness of Puck in a poem,
to have the spectacle of dissolving in a snowflake,
to have a sense of the history of flickering in candlelight,
to have views of Monet's Rouen Cathedral façades in
        changing light,
to see your genuine expression in what seems to be
        varied illumination
that's been a long time fortunate pastime of mine.

*We were in Rouen a few days ago, and here I am in front of the
1892 Painting of the Cathedral at the End of the Day; magic
transformation by light and the light of Monet's soul makes this
into a very warm gentle lyric, no hard grey stone, pale pink and
pale yellow and at the bottom and top pale blue, all vibrant, all a
personal lyric.*

Claude Monet
ROUEN CATHEDRAL
1892
Musée Marmottan, Paris

Resounding   Resounding   Resounding
Ocean waves too do that
and Desperado Dylan Thomas' poetry
Resounding Many Waves of Sound Expanding
like billions of Hindus saying OM.
But now the Great Organ is Resounding
in La Cattedrale di Rouen, more than once
Monet made it resound softly in varied blues
and greys in the music of his bearded reverence,
old prophet, new testaments each time the sun
touched upon the façade of the rich textured church.

The poet responds to the cathedral
itself, not to a painting, but is
reminded of Monet's paintings

Portail de la Cathédrale de Rouen temps gris

Door of the Cathedral, grey blue,
      touched upon
by snowflakes, angels, Monet,
      he knows
his, our snowflakes and everywhere light of
      angels, also
in sleep flowers and butterflies emerging from
      his beard,
he eats some bread, gets out of bed,
      cooperates
with the changing weather, changing seasons,
      transforms
transforms; now I know the façade as seen
      through the
radiant blue joyous work prayers of a
      blessing master.

Claude Monet
Portail de la Cathédrale de Rouen temps gris
1894
Musée des Beaux-Arts, Rouen

Just a little bit of the distant somewhat
cloudy bright sky is seen
in the agitated light blue horizon

When Appreciation agitates the various
          tones of the green and
blue rhythmic sea by agitated long enduring
          receptive some high
upstanding rocks, they are as agitated as
          upgrown odd
hardy upsurging blossoms, various dark colors
          in the those dense
rocks, when appreciation brings us agitated
          together in this
coastal oceanic scene (the ocean itself like a
          symphony),
when this Happens along with me and Monet
          you're in for a Holiday!
          cool too!

Claude Monet
LES PYRAMIDES DE PORT-COTON
1886
formerly Rau Foundation
Seen at a special exhibit in the Musée du Luxembourg, Paris, 2000

Maisons dans la neige en Norvège

How much you love weather, changing
        weather!
poet of painting! musician of moving tones!
        now, here's a
snowfall, now here's a blizzard of light and
        snow,
weather, weather, my companion through life and
        poetry,
I hear Wordsworth talking to daffodils, I hear
        you with
your brush uplifted brushing up on learning;
        O blizzard
O blizzard, how I take you to my heart like a
        wave of ecstasy!

Claude Monet
MAISONS DANS LA NEIGE EN NORVÈGE
1895
formerly Rau Foundation
Seen at a special exhibit in the Musée du Luxembourg, Paris, 2000

Notes while in the Musée de l'Orangerie, Paris

*But now to go again to the last operas of Monet…Les Nymphéas,
the large curving Waterlilies Series. Now be religious, now do
Debussy, now do Virginia Woolf's The Waves. Now be a sustained
epic of belief. Now see what you can see. Now Be. In the morning
it was those 2 Rose Windows of Notre Dame and then a great
time walking in crowded streets with holiday crowds in the
gardens of the Tuileries. And now just before the museum closes the
two oval shaped rooms with the lyrical epics of Monet. It is before
leaving Paris a way of Thanking God, isn't it?*

Nymphéas, Effet du Soir

Small wide cups of flickering flames on the altar
and here on the Giverny Pond
white water lilies

a floating expansive pleasure
reverence of Monet

1897

Claude Monet
LES NYMPHÉAS
1897
Musée de l'Orangerie, Paris

Monet scenes of fields,
here many yellow flowers in the wind

As a matter of vibrant fields, of flickering
        pale flowers petals in
the soft blue green world, vague soft puffs of
        extended light clouds
above. As a matter of fact he makes us continue to
        experience this now.

Le Pont Japonais

Amorphous and amore
richness of foliage above below
and surrounding the Japanese bridge
soaked in the sleepiness and music
of Debussy and Monet
                1918-24

La Barque

Dark greenish dark blue water

Biding time
        slightly swaying rowboat
                by thick grass in water   cornered
                   by a Monet dream
                       1887

Claude Monet
Inspired by images including Le Pont Japonais, La Barque
1887 - 1924
Musée Marmottan, Paris

Notes: Pablo Picasso

This work for centuries will make many people smile, will convey comedy, tragedy, energy... long live Odysseus! long live the Mediterranean energy and joy creating composer! enterprising Odysseus Picasso amazes; never mind theorizing about Zen; Picasso just keeps going...champion bicyclists have nothing on him...he speeds, keeps constructing, giving us energy and pleasure. A hero with a thousand faces, with more than a thousand compositions. Long Live the Free Artist! nourishing our energies for the future!

It can be in ways a problem for a reader if a writer is abundantly prolific and a problem for a visitor if a painter is tremendously facile and prolific. Facile? if it is really good, esthetic, meaningful, then most likely it is not facile for many – only for Mozart and other geniuses. The reader or viewer has to choose, take a little at a time, give enough contemplation. If one tries to read most of Shakespeare in one week there may be problems; if one tries to see too much Picasso in one or a few days – also problems. But these are not faults in the creators. This huge place full of hundreds of Picasso paintings contains only a little part of his work.

PICASSO! a long lifetime of construction, of ingenuity, of energy and invention, an Odysseus of a traveler in art, prolific creator of images, energies, that continue. Comedy, Tragedy, Zest, Continuity, Playful Energy Giving Continuity. Critics can judge and mumble all they want. But Picasso gives us more life, more life, aware of Guernica and tragedy, but finally an Odysseus giving us More Life!

Sometimes no "message" or belief other than expression, design, entertaining forms, the grand joy and comedy of that; vitality of ingenuity and construction, art for exuberance's sake. Thousands of lesser than Picasso artists have continued in clichés and staleness of so called novelty and experimentation, inevitable; but then one has to decide is vitality and ingenuity enough for me?

Musée Picasso, Paris

Picasso Self-Portrait

Today a stance is fine
        as long
as it is temporary or else one becomes
            cemented
fixed – so here young Picasso
            stares
towards his desired future determined
            to be
unswerved from his Necessity, from changing
            fulfillment
after fulfillment, canvas after canvas; so he
            goes
strongly vividly strongly on painting for more
        than 80 years.

Pablo Picasso
SELF-PORTRAIT, *detail*
1901
Musée Picasso, Paris

Pablo Picasso
HARLEQUIN
1901
Metropolitan Museum of Art, New York

216

The world is curved; is
The Word curved?

Space is curved,
the body of the clown pensive
painted by Picasso is curved;
the petals behind him and the women
sometimes thought of by him are curved;
care is curved and sometimes caressing;
C in the words celestial and caring is curved
Circus and Comedy can also be curved; as a matter
of decorative and pleasing design there is
pleasure and care for curves in this
1901 turn of the century painting
by sometimes playful
Picasso.

Great helpful white wide sails or "Ulysse et les Sirènes"
or Ship tossed, wind tossed, world whirled,
secure Picasso/Odysseus

Tie me to this mast, this mass, this world,
bind me to time so I may hear these ultra violet sounds,
      mermaids, sirens, voices of winds, messages,
      sounds from old stones, all countries
      all objects, hold me fast to
this bed of conception, this ship of rhyme, so that I might
      see all islands, women, dolphins in
      musical commotion. Hear
the whistling and wishes of fishes, see the winds become blue skies
      I said it, I want all histories, all
      stories in song; I want to return
      with them to you, Penelope.

Pablo Picasso
Ulysse et les Sirènes
1946-1947
Musée Picasso, Antibes

NOTES: Picasso's Sculpture

*Anatomy of Le verre d'absinthe…anatomy of a violin…
anatomy of a cello…anatomy of a guitar…anatomy of a Tête
de femme and of Tête d'homme…As an artist the important
question is what do you really feel like making – what do you
have to make, what demand is making you really make it? and
then go ahead. Picasso's zest conviction that art is play, more
than conviction, necessary practice of play as art.. Picasso with
non-stop zest, with whim and bronze.*

Tête de Femme, Bronze

Something to contend with
to realize as rugged complex
a cliff to climb to behold
to assert   to hold   comprehend and
create if you can

Pablo Picasso
TÊTE DE FEMME
1959
Seen at a special exhibition of Picasso's sculpture, Centre Pompidou, Paris, 2000

Guitar

Guitar
to take you apart
musically guitar
to take you apart thoughtfully
playfully making music of the process
makes me an architect of music
now you can comprehend
and dance

Pablo Picasso
GUITAR, SCULPTURE
1912-1913
Seen at a special exhibition of Picasso's sculpture
Centre Pompidou, Paris

Homme à la Mandoline

Man in and of the Mandoline.
Mandoline in and of the man in the music of
elaborate
construction cubist part by part, time by time,
of the
assembled design, do I see you? do I design you?
Yes, I guess
my dizzy definite aim is construction, is music.

Pablo Picasso
HOMME À LA MANDOLINE
1911
Seen at a special exhibition of Picasso's sculpture, Centre Pompidou, Paris, 2000

Woman in White

To be
but not to assert, to be fully here, receptive, listening,
          in repose
but not to be willful; female principle in classic white,
          repose, aware of
breeze; aware of everything in space by letting it go;
          sustained affectionate
pregnancy; womb of the cosmos-and-Imagination; listening
          in almost emptiness,
biding time and when she and he are ready
          Apollo is born. Or
          again heard from.

Pablo Picasso
WOMAN IN WHITE
1923
Museum of Modern Art, New York

Pablo Picasso
LES DEMOISELLES D'AVIGNON
1907
Museum of Modern Art, New York

222

Les Demoiselles d'Avignon

We are such things as crystals are made of
    and cliffs and stars and polyps
    and star fish, as rhythms in
    ice, the faces of geological
    ages; stages in the
growing of strong trees, different Aspects of a
    Self. We are as ephemeral
    as the cosmos, consorts
    of Prospero or Picasso.

Baigneuses Regardant un Avion

On the Picasso Riviera the fat fine nude gals are
        calm and distended,
two are in the water, reader, put your head under for a while,
        wet and extended;
to what extent are you erotic and Mediterranean and
        controlled and
contemplative? put your brush again and again
        in different colors,
compose heavenly thighs, begin to sign where troubadours
        expended their sperm.
I almost forgot that it was Summer and that the
        five wonderous upgazing gals
        were looking at the beginning
        of flight and language.

Pablo Picasso
Baigneuses Regardant un Avion
1920
Musée Picasso, Paris

Story of Adam

Old Adam
with his white beard
already knew about Hiroshima and
    me and you,
he had harvested grapes with Piero's
    uncle, and
sedate, dignified, tired, worldly-wise
    posed for him;
was thought of later by Cézanne and often by
    me and you;
bone-wise ancient father, you tell us
    don't slump,
get to work, we and our cousins have made
    a mess of it,
now, get to whatever work enacts the love
    of our descendent
who will be deceived, betrayed, die at
    the crossroad.
Piero, you keep your cool, you take us
    to the mystic
school of mathematics in painting. You work
    beautifully having
absorbed, among other things, the mercy of the
    sky of Arezzo.

Piero della Francesca
STORY OF ADAM, FRESCO
1448
Church of San Francesco, Arezzo

A reverent look at different kinds of students, prophets, surgeons, others....

Naturally I know that to write about the designs, colors, compositions of these Great Rembrandt Paintings requires years of care and praise; I appreciate the paintings in those terms and some of the studies of them but my task is of a different kind. The thoughts of the scientists at the Anatomy Lesson and good scholars analyzing Rembrandt's skill have different degrees of enlightenment to be respected.

Rembrandt van Rijn
THE ANATOMY LESSON
1656
Rijksmuseum, Amsterdam

The Anatomy Lesson

A life of Study. Study Christ Crucified and all related
        to that.
And study the body of Everyman – in all humility,
        in all
precision and perseverance and pursue one muscle to
        another, one
blood vessel to another, the organization of all
        organs,
learn to help mankind, all tributaries leading
        to the heart.
The heartfelt thought of Rembrandt leading to
        his
Anatomy Lesson and other biblical works.

Rembrandt van Rijn
THE JEWISH BRIDE
1665
Rijksmuseum, Amstserdam

The Jewish Bride or
The incomparable gold of the marriage of true minds

What can be touched? what can be known?
What can be protected? how can one protect?
       a certain look
protects; the greatest strength based on the purest
       gentleness;
no jewels and no clothes can equal the mystery of her
       authenticity;
the husband aware as can be of the rarity of that
       beauty, her
kind of authenticity, wishes to be an author praising
       it; to praise

Jeremiah

Jeremiah
in loneliness
his old tired almost bald almost sleeping
      head
Illuminated, in darkness a stream of light by
      his feet and
side. How pensive and lonely can one be so as
      to go
beyond the forlorn – to where the world was
      born!

Rembrandt van Rijn
JEREMIAH
1630
Rijksmuseum, Amsterdam

The Abduction of Europa

The manuals and books of science tell us some about this;
        what is it all about,
cosmic sex, the preconditioned Zeus, she (and
        all the world?)
being carried away to? she who holds on for dear life,
        (dear? dangerous?)
necessary life. The white pleased compelled bull, god,
        wets his feet,
splashes in success, seduction, who is seduced? and where
        are they going?

Rembrandt van Rijn
THE ABDUCTION OF EUROPA
1632
J. Paul Getty Museum, Los Angeles

231

Research-and-Recreation

Being dramatic about the dramatic about the most
        dramatic
Rembrandt-and-Bible are big-and-dramatic at that;
        passion
suffering salvation tragedy ecstasy are not
        minimized,
Mystery not belittled, the value of value, of faith,
        of life
not for a chiaroscuro moment minimized. Value
        increases
by the help of Isaiah, Genesis, reverence,
        Rembrandt.

For me these Rembrandt paintings are often prophetic,
teach me more of life and Christianity than pages in the Bible.

Certainly Rembrandt's rereading of the Bible made him see all of
his subjects with the profoundest compassion.

Yvonne et Christine Lerolle au Piano

Let me listen,
let me help you turn a page,
you are at the piano making music, I can
        slightly read
music, somewhat understand, completely to my
        particular moment
meaning my kind of temporal infinity love you
        making music.
Renoir wrote the score. Debussy listened in.
        You in the Orangerie
of the Tuileries twittered a tune; let me listen.

Pierre-Auguste Renoir
YVONNE ET CHRISTINE LEROLLE AU PIANO, *detail*
1897
Musée de l'Orangerie, Paris

233

Pierre-Auguste Renoir
MONET PAINTING IN ARGENTEUIL
1873
Wadsworth Atheneum Museum of Art, Hartford, CT

234

Autobiographies blossom; or
Renoir paints Monet working in his garden in Argenteuil

It will slightly control me as I try to control it,
        it surprises us,
the wet top of my brush as I glance at bushes and blossoms
        behind a fence,
as I imagine a lingerer or listener in my dream, colors
        in vibration,
as I receive, look, as I make, wet dab of paint by
        wet dab of surprise,
words occur within the leaves; the closed or open shutters of
        the nearby house please
as your eyes do closing or opening as you smile, as you
        desire. My stance is as steady
as one excited can be as I again wet the tip of the somewhat
        magic brush. You say:
hush, continue painting, hold the rainbow in your arm, near
        your heart; results will be
        a garden and a painting.

Claude Renoir as Clown

Look – my son as a clown and I as a
          clown and
you as a clown realize that masks and
          paintings are necessary,
so if my sentences hope for comedy let that
          wet your appetite,
let your sense easily without frenzy or propaganda
          become pleasantly very
alert. Repose is necessary for the fulfillment of the rose. Women
          and humor can help.

Pierre-Auguste Renoir
CLAUDE AS A CLOWN
1909
Musée de l'Orangerie, Paris

Pierre-Auguste Renoir's wife was a bit off key and they were
          both scraping carrots,
all was colorful and fine in this world; she sort of continues
          her off-key song,
he displayed his joyful thankfulness in his body, her
          body, the
vegetables and colors of the world by lifting his brush, shaking
          his brush,
touching again and again and again, all was celebration, his
          new canvas.

Jean Renoir (son of Pierre-Auguste Renoir)
recollects a scene with his parents
which inspired this poem by J. T.

La petite fée des eaux

Now here's water flowing off the back
Of a bare assed lovely woman crouching
In a low tub of water; a dove comes down
To take a dip; lip to lip, merging
In wetness until the fluency of love becomes our nature.

Auguste Rodin
La Petite Fée des Eaux, sculpture
1903
Musée Rodin, Paris

NOTES: Auguste Rodin

The Convalescent...seems to be emerging from the bedrock, the sea of marble; what necessitated the stone, what necessitated the sculptor's Imagination necessitates slowly her recovery...In many of the marble images, so much merging and emerging...And for me much that brings Debussy to mind.

Le Sommeil...yin and yang; Rodin is especially good at creating the essence of stillness, silence, sleep, – and creating a rhythmic sense of fluency, activity of rippling effects, light and darkness.

Michelangelo's Captives or Prisoners struggle strongly emerging from stone; Rodin's gentle Aurora emerges from stone, she with the soft lips, she with a desire to be fully awakened by the creative eye, love, of the creator; she who slowly awakens the youth in the dawn.

I was just looking at the Portrait of Père Eymard; when bronze can become flame; when 23 year old Rodin's Image can predict its subject's future-and-fame...And then there are wonderful Portraits of sensual aristocratic intelligent smiling women. Free of the Christian condemnation.

Bronze sketches related to Balzac

Balzac
Balzac
you old tough rugged fat Bloke
fertile big balls, novel after novel after
novel, not pot boilers but furnaces concerning
lust greed money business ego madness the rough
volcanic material, mind and society in motion, hypocrisy,
ruthless; bloke of the brave pen night after night
drinking coffee writing giving populations of
characters the Works.

Auguste Rodin
Balzac: Nude Study
1892-93
Musée Rodin, Paris

238

Le Navire dans la Tempête

A boat is in a sea of wavering wandering
            varied dark
green Henri Rousseau waves and it is also a
            house of many
dreamers in the rain. There is a little French flag.
            Now this painter
is an old and delighted captain who takes us
            to safety.

Henri Rousseau
Le Navire dans la Tempête
1890
Musée de l'Orangerie, Paris

John Singer Sargent
La Carmencita
1892
Musée d'Orsay, Paris

La Carmencita

Giving him a stance, a glance,
a chance to be opulent, the proud beauty,
      Spanish dancer, says
Come on, American noble Sargent, splurge, we
      have the urge
to come together; someday millions will see us
      when we are
gone and say they are here to stay, their stance and
      glance always
      starts music.

A Young Maidservant

The way your modest glance, the way you
        turn towards
any object, subject, beginning of a butterfly
        or universe or
even me is enough to make even the traveling
        moon seem to be
a minor mystery, very effective; the way
        you are pensive
and observant brings civilization and music
        into evidence.
You know how fragile everything is, even
        cliffs and
sea surges; you listen to a pebble, you
        so regard a
person as to make prophets seem limited.

Michael Sweerts
A YOUNG MAIDSERVANT
1660
Seen at a special exhibition of the paintings of Michael Sweerts
at the Wadsworth Atheneum Museum of Art, Hartford, CT, 2002

Portrait of a Melancholy Young Man

Why are you melancholy?
Why are we melancholy? not comfortable
        outside the womb?
not cozy and assured of the everything to be
        discovered? world.
My remote ancestor, where did I come from and
        why? Was there
a time when ocean, moon, sun, all all were one?

So we have coins? So we had dreams, desires,
        ambitions,
temporarily, touched upon what we thought we desired.

Michael Sweerts
PORTRAIT OF A YOUNG MAN
1656
Seen at a special exhibition of the paintings of Michael Sweerts
at the Wadsworth Atheneum Museum of Art, Hartford, CT, 2002

Saint Sebastian

And so the wounded gold lit almost naked hero is bent over,
     arrows piercing him,
the illuminated ones in this chiaroscuro drama, the turbaned
     women are caring for
the wounded saint, trying to remove the arrows; here no
     narcissus but
charity; the wounded (dying?) youth has served his
     Cause, is being
served by those capable of care, affection.

Hendrick Ter Brugghen
Saint Sebastian tended by Irene
1625
Allen Memorial Art Museum, Oberlin, Ohio

L'Archangelo Raffaele e Tobio

Be a delicate stepping angel
      and
take that child's hand, any child!
      how
privileged you will be, how educated, uplifted
      we
will be; be a clear minded faithful very
      wide
winged angel and take this child's hand,
      any
child, see how it will guide you. Eden
      is again
Eventually Possible. Paradise is found again.
      When my
mother squeezed my hand the day before she
      died
was I not forever transported?

Titian
Tobias and the Angel
date unknown
San Marciliano, Venice

245

Titian
VENUS OF URBINO
1538
Uffizi Gallery, Florence

La Venere di Urbino and Surroundings

Extended beauty,
reclining Venus, Italy Imagined by Tiziano, we touch
        upon that lightly,
with color in poems and paintings, with vows in vowels
        and verbs;
the extended beauty harmoniously receptive and presentable is there
        is here for us to see;
such Visions and such Being bring about Urbino and music's revision
        in our continuing hope.

Miranda notices Turner and is established in Wonder:
"You oft began to tell me who I am"

Did you ever see a
world in a soap bubble
if so you have a fine
perspective to view and celebrate
Lichfield Cathedral by the
reappearing magician Turner;
instructed by Prospero in
the Tempest to take a turn
or two, to make the world
appear again for Miranda,
he continued the watercolor
way of Praise; O Brave, new
world that has such sketches in it.

J. M. W. Turner
LICHFIELD CATHEDRAL
1830-35
Location Unknown

Saint George overcomes the Dragon

You couldn't have a more decorative dragon
expanded expended and gorgeous in art. St. George
subdues him with a touch of Uccello which means
the dragon becomes an extravaganza, St. George
is pleased and skillful at amusement and ease like
Paolo Uccello.

Paolo Uccello
SAINT GEORGE AND THE DRAGON
1470
National Gallery, London

Paolo Uccello
The Battle of San Romano
1454-7
National Gallery, London

250

The Battle of San Romano

This is the way it should be....Battaglia Battaglia
contemplated unto decoration, picturesque unto
festival, horses rearing to the tune of Uccello's
bird calls, amusement of lances and prances, armor
that is related to the author's armor, scattered
helmets that make a game of shapes; victory couldn't
be better. Oranges by the dark leaves.

Vincent van Gogh
OLIVE ORCHARD
1889
Van Gogh Museum, Amsterdam

Every path of changing light is the Way

You can take this
　　　　　path
　　　　　or that path
　　　　　in the olive orchard
or mesmerized walk down any aisle of
　　　　　the church or asylum
songs from early childhood come back to participate
　　　　　with the baffled dreamer
there are streams meandering by in which spots of blood
　　　　　might be seen,
a cave loses its door, poppies by the edge of life
　　　　　repeat only
consummatum est, the blue shadows of the leaves
　　　　　of the olive trees
remind us of those vortices where the lovers
　　　　　leapt into the Sea

NOTE:

*Yes, Picasso is energetic stupendous extraordinary –
but my need for religious blossoming leads me to the
extravagance of the charity of Whitman and Van Gogh.*

God's Fool (or A Corner of the Asylum Garden)

A little corner of the
                    asylum garden,
It is as vast as the world, it goes on
                    and on to all words,
an angel dancing on a pin's head is bigger than
                    we are in our second of burning
                    in this fertile field of saints,
                    beggars, the sick;
who dares to say – good   bad   sick   normal
                    insane   saved   gone?
perhaps changed, see some spots of blood, see some
                    Keats and van Gogh and Monet
                    signs of prayer,
we stagger on the stones, knees bruised in that sacred
                    way, companions to
                    Lear and Gloucester and
he who goes to sleep at Noon.

Vincent van Gogh
CORNER OF THE ASYLUM GARDEN
1889
Van Gogh Museum, Amsterdam

Yellow House in Arles

By seeing it this way
this yellow house is now my house,
    I proclaim it
to my soul (and those listening in), no other
    cry or color
equals this; this is my cared for yellow house that
    I invite you into.

Vincent van Gogh
Yellow House in Arles
1888
Van Gogh Museum, Amsterdam

255

The Sower with the Setting Sun

Humus and Consortium

Trees slant towards me,
I slant towards them, the dancing world is
      heavy material
and I am heavy material and light though
      on it, the Sun's light
thought us out, it is hugely whirling as I
      cast the seeds, they
fall to the earth like the games of angels,
      propelling me the
whirling enormous sun with its millions of flames
      is speaking to the inside
of a seed; every seed receives its co-existence,
      infinitesimal and grandiose,
repeated turns of earth and sun; sheep hear the rumbling.
      Housewives know it's gone on
for centuries. Yet the sower urged this way or that way
      by matter and star
is no longer separate from the seeds he flings than
      light is from dust, or death from life.
      Where will he put his body in need
      of rest tonight? Can the
      universe find any kind of
      coziness? the cosmos
and the insect in the long plumed weeds consorting in a dance.

Vincent van Gogh
THE SOWER
1888
Van Gogh Museum, Amsterdam

The Wings fan the Fires

I sway,
I kneel anyway, the ship is going down, going round,
look the bed is extended, is moving, the baton or the paintbrush
        or the magician's needs
consume our molecules; the floor is the door; the sky is the
        wall; the straw chairs
the stairs the stars the fires; Arles, are you still on
        fire? Van Gogh was at the
green window; you heard angels wrestling.

Vincent van Gogh
ROOM IN ARLES
1889
Van Gogh Museum, Amsterdam

An 1888 harvest admired in 2000 and so on

Haystacks for me, as great and perennial as pyramids;
    I like their
shape, warmth, gold; an ant better than a pharaoh
    is snug,
is protected, in one. Bees fly over the golden and
    green fields.

Vincent van Gogh
THE HARVEST
1888
Van Gogh Museum, Amsterdam

Enclosed Field with Plowman

How much can you plough
              determined by the
              planetary system and
              your parents and ancestors,
              ploughman? how
much can you turn up, seed, sing, can you bring
              visions to the vagina
              of the earth, to
ocean waves of the sacred earth, from its symphonies, from
              its undulations,
from its furrows, further and further and further Mysteries,
              from its yielding,
from its readiness? a temporary, strong as must be, marked,
              momentary ploughman
near his tiny house with his obedient dark horse go about
              their seasonal work,
planting; the round full whirling sacred large beguiled
              travelling speaking
Sun is in its sky in its Golden Age; every one has
              a Path

Vincent van Gogh
ENCLOSED FIELD WITH PLOWMAN
1889
Private Collection

Self-Portrait mostly in blue, at Saint-Rémy

Friends, world citizens, countrymen, lend me your ears,
       you see this one
is gone, you see He is bandaged nailed He is naked known
       by every child
and by every dying man, woman; wait, I must paint
       my few scenes as
you stagger on our Via Crucis; look, the paintbrush
       paints by Itself,
It takes the sky in hand, why all that swishing in
       the Word, why do
you continue to stare to stare to stare at all the
       suffering in the world?

Vincent van Gogh
SELF PORTRAIT
1889
Van Gogh Museum, Amsterdam

1890…year of his death.. Landscape at Twilight

How can it be but it is
that one man – one life can give itself (and us)
> away
so generously…the phases of his brief life so profound,
> so genuine,
so changing, so vibrant. Twilight. Turbulence.
> Pity and Terror.
The Sky all yellow in Commotion. The swift narrow
> country path.
The blades of grass like saints on fire. "Unless
> a man loses
his life he will not find it" or us. So
> evangelists bow.

Vincent van Gogh
LANDSCAPE WITH THE CHATEAU OF AUVERS AT SUNSET
1890
Van Gogh Museum, Amsterdam

Johannes Vermeer
THE MILKMAID IN THE KITCHEN
1658
Rijksmuseum, Amsterdam

The Milkmaid in the Kitchen

So
she is doing
just what the Bhagavad-Gita says and what
        I try to
remind myself to do every day of the year: Perform
        every action
sacramentally and be free from all attachments to results.
        A chore?
An accepted routine. Religion on the domestic scale,
        compact
with obedience. Vermeer quietly selectively carefully
        acknowledging
values, the essentials, good bread, milk, service,
        patience, steadiness,
shadows in the acceptance of destiny, the milk is
        poured. Modesty
and service make her and her pure imagist as
        successful as can be.

The Glass of Wine

What is being proposed? what is being toasted? some light
      from outside is
an annunciation of her purity and Vermeer's; what is the
      large hatted
merchant planning? What I know is that Vermeer's use of
      light and his
reverence like an angel of the annunciation protects her
      purity forever;
the delicate regard for her and light convinces of an
      immediate
protection; there is a plan and pattern to all this,
      there is a
luminous and transparent glass of wine; an object held
      in such regard
becomes a chalice; if we are sometimes innocent fools
      thank God.

Johannes Vermeer
THE GLASS OF WINE
1658-60
State Museum, Berlin

IV

20TH - CENTURY PAINTERS & SCULPTORS
IN THE UNITED STATES

I practice this belief of tradition and the individual talent as I go from book to book, from painting to painting, from country to country. As to the consequences I'm not going to try to judge that. I find freshness, recreation, in these classic paintings. I remember what Ezra Pound felt about a classic; it is a classic not because it conforms to certain structural rules…but because of a certain eternal and inexpressible freshness.

NOTES: Marsden Hartley

Spirit of the Place....
and/or a Mystic Geography?
Expressionist and Symbolist
– his scenes of Maine or
New Mexico or France are
not so much scenes of places
(that after all he didn't really
"belong" to) but scenes of
states of mind that possessed
him. As in the work of other
symbolists – Poe, Baudelaire
– they are landscapes of the
psyche. So actually Marsden
"the Man from Maine" according to the emphasis of some of the
biographies is not so much giving us "local color" of Maine scenes
(Schoodic Point, etc.) but it's more like the "dark night of the
soul" or the cold and turbulent "sea of troubles" of the psyche –
(the war within, the den of Mars? And this reminds me of the
bold and effective Military Insignia of the Berlin Paintings.)

Alfred Stieglitz
MARSDEN HARTLEY
1915-1916
Museum of Modern Art, New York

266

And once more the rhythmic ritual sunset waves
        of the pointed hard triumphant
          sea repeats its
chorus, its great tragic chorus, its grave secrets
        with the most delicious
          word death,
Speaks it to the ear and pen and brush stroke of
        the sad prophet
          Marsden.
Do not weaken, Reader, do not mar his work.
        "Mark Me"
says the Prophet dying and triumphing into the night.

Poem inspired by his painting – Storm Clouds –
and the Portrait of Hartley by the photographer Alfred Stieglitz.

I have seen the death of the sea gull
      the coming of the storm
      the heavy weight of
      the breaking wave
and the lost swimmer off the rocky shore,
the slow burning in dust of the mill cities,
the millions of years of unenlightenment, the indifference
      in the lost walkers, those unable
      to see or sing the sun,
that naked boy beats against the rocks and sea weeds, a few days before he was
      reading
      Whitman; and so
aware of the storm clouds and heavy and brooding in
      search of beauty
I take my moveable melancholy, my stance and moveable canvases
      and so, dear lover, in the
      unknown future
I hope you hear the whispered word, beyond "Nevermore,"
      beyond the storm, over the fertile desiring
      rich dark mountain, my brother.

Marsden Hartley
Storm Clouds, Maine Scene
1906-1907
Walker Art Center, Minneapolis

Marsden Hartley
PORTRAIT OF A GERMAN OFFICER
1914
Metropolitan Museum of Art, New York

Prizes uniting soldier-and-lover

What do you make of me – Insignia? – turmoil and decor,
      military
lover and strong paint, celebration of motion; and design
      coming to grips
with a Prussian passion. Warriors. Military Emblems.
      Horses. Pageants.
Collisions of regiments. Fanfare of medals. Play and Submission
      with the power of
Abstraction; Color; constructing out of the paraphernalia of lust
      and parades and war the
      victories of a painter.

Suggested by Hartley's abstract paintings of German military officers.

271

Marsden Hartley
THREE MEN STANDING BEHIND TWO SEATED WOMEN WITH APRONS
a study for FISHERMAN'S FAMILY, 1943
Bates College Museum of Art, Lewiston, ME

272

Fisherman's Family

A shattering.

Cumbersome and sinking.

After the storm the dead plovers. After lightening and dead lovers.
      The huge bodies of the two boys
heavy and washed up. The wharf disintegrating and a wreck.
      The heavy old hands on the
canvas long after the Fall of Rome in bleak Maine towns. Far
      from the Mediterranean and
far far from Tiepolo and any enlightening melody; there the large
      belief and Italy inflates the body
to celestial opera, sensual and opulence; Venice, there it is
      natural for the supernatural to have
spirit uplift body, sensuous body in large harmonies; Venus and Adonis
      here the decaying wharf, the lumber
going to pieces, greyness, coldness; the fishermen's family loses
      its two sons; the families and
      towns become ghosts.

Marsden Hartley
THE LOST FELICE
1939
Los Angeles County Museum of Art

The Lost Felice

There There like a white Ghost like the Mother of the
        Moon like an old old old
French Proverb turned into old old Canadian fantasy
        The Mother,
hulk, bulk, boldness of substantial presence, how many
        Quebec winters, how many
North Atlantic Seas, how many lost uncles and
        sea captains, there there
Stunned in the eternal Present, abiding by her kitchen
        Chores, smells of Fish and God,
routine of death and birth, the woman in her bridal
        gown and funeral gown and dress made of
        the light of the brightest
Moon, continues her work, faces the sea, faces the
        darkness, faces the death of
        all people.

Fisherman's Last Supper

The three empty chairs: Father, Son, and Holy Ghost;
Marsden and the two young fishermen who died at sea,
      the three of them unseen;
the empty chairs wait for all the contemplatives,
      those who study the petals in the eyes
      of the Passion Fish, those who muse,
      ponder, pray confronting the strong
      French-Canadian Family, bread,
      sacrament, life-and-death.
A star and wish governing each person; the contemplative
      studies the skull; the painter
shows the Scene: Rocks, Death, the Human Family
      breaking the bread.

Marsden Hartley
FISHERMAN'S LAST SUPPER
1938
Private Collection, NY

Paintings by John Marin
seen at the Portland Museum of Art, Portland, Maine

Necessities Joining or Rejoicing

    Knowing what you wanted
        you know what I wanted
        knowing via the music and dance
        of color what you and I wanted.

        Maine be my Metaphor
            if the Mariner
            were literary
        Marin might have said, but amidst
            coolness wind and light
        the adventurer imagined via watercolors.

Remote, near, Responsive governors

    Not
    ashes to ashes
    but
    freshness to freshness
    coolness of the almost free mind
    to coolness of the almost free breeze and ocean.

Two poems based on sculpture by Marianna Pineda

Twirling

Whirled into
the spinning world like delicate
    and
vulnerable planets, two young girls are
    holding hands;
feet to feet, freshness and elation to
    freshness and
elation-capable and twirling, pensive
    and at play,
daughters of Wonder and Air they form
    a V,
high symbols of a to be protected
    victory.

Marianna Pineda
Twirling
1975
Summer Street Housing for the Elderly, East Boston, MA
Courtesy Boston Art Commission 2014

The Sleepwalker

The sleepwalker
The deep walker
urged to feel the night air
to move as the child in the womb
     moves its
body to touch the universe to say let
     me be in
your world to look at you who slept and awoke
once the womb of your mother, way back
     to the
first Eve, my needs and feelings are not
     blind,
but in this dangerous world I walking knowing
     that the
chance to see your eyes and the moon and stars
     and the
daytime miracle of world and birth might be
     missed,
I walk tentatively, I feel the air, read its
     messages,
I have a calling, I hear music that is
     distant,
I believe my future child is the musician
     saying walk,
     talk to me,
     listen.

Marianna Pineda
THE SLEEPWALKER
1951
Private Collection

Responses to paintings by Mark Rothko

What magic does a color do to you
What music does a color do to you
are you blue are you black are you
back where rain began a rainbow
where pain partly mastered for some days
begins a painting? to be dazed amazed
you have this sacred rage for order

The body-and-soul is a center of influences, reacting at
times to tones of sound, tones of color, sensations
of heat and cold, mugginess or clarity, to slowness
and speed, what a wonder that we can take it all…
and that we can compose art and interpretations
responding to these sensations…and transform
them into personal lyrics and meanings, sending
out our own vibrations and colors

The vibrations that come from the qualities of light, the tones and the meanings of colors, can only be received when confronting the original and not a photograph (or a comment!). One derives power and blessing from absorbing the light from the best stained glass windows - and from organizations that I imagine as transcending some pain and struggle; whatever the case may be they aggrandize and enact a field of celebration.

Not numbered   not titled
the grain of sand   the paintings of
Rothko the shadows that come from
your hands and the colors that
come from his mind   an expanse
like a horizon   a series of movements
as in a sonata   measurements
order   as in mathematics   he
wonders what to do with his life   or
his death   this is a need for and
a Way of   Composing

Paintings by Mark Rothko
dates unknown
Seen at the Museum of Modern Art, New York

Betty Woodman
IL GIARDINO DIPINTO, *detail*
1993
RISD Museum, Providence

Il Giardino Dipinto

These dancers

these figures on a balustrade

these antic upstanding in profile playful

figures of a ceramic well organized cool fantasy parade

they please   they proceed   they show off   their gestures

vases   O   vases   vases   O   vases   reversals

and   advancements   yes   the   music   advances   advances

if Balanchine would see this   he would be most delighted

on the balcony   by the balustrade

did   you   say   light?

Yes   light   atmosphere

space-choreography   hereby please   as often

so   does   Italy   repeat   as   does   Italy

our Italy   as so do flowers   yes   flowers

Fiesole   Betty lived near us and one of Gertrude Stein's places

Il Giardino Dipinto   Veramente

a delight of color   fanfare   flare   notes of music

and expert acrobats   could not be better

we are delighted   we are enlightened

we are thankful

Poem written while looking at Betty Woodman's Ceramic Installation

Surf,
moonlit full breasted risen one,
nice loose bush of hair, great splurge of sea,
these waves of action overwhelm us, eventually
we are born, all along we are borne
by tides and thighs, night is
aroused, enters by the
way of Desire

Andrew Wyeth
Rocks and the Sea
1944
Farnsworth Art Museum, Rockland, Maine

Transparency is excellent
especially if you have that cool body
        those breasts
those nipples to show   mermaid
        or muse or
wet woman   of course I wonder
        where I am
you seem awfully pleased after that
        dip
naked you come ashore   I suppose
        the birth of Venus
has always been   somewhat unknown
        somewhat untitled

some of us must paint and faint, have
        a faint notion
through the transparency of a stream or dream
        of the reality of
        that nudity

Andrew Wyeth
COMING ASHORE
1991
Farnsworth Art Museum, Rockland, Maine

Adrift

Lulled asleep
like a Viking? like a New Englander bearded
in ancient times, going as always from one world to another,
singular noted revered voyager by the vast field of ocean
vast field of sky
the moment
no matter how adrift
how asleep or awake you are is
the new found land

Andrew Wyeth
ADRIFT
1982
Collection of the Artist

Bettered and Battered I am not Broken

Well I've plundered a few thousand paintings in my Day,
        treasures of the Louvre,
treasures of love, treasures of the Uffizi, treasures of the
        Vatican, treasures
of the vacations in the Metropolitan and Elsewhere
        East and West,
the best is where you find-and-make it; now
        here I am by
silent exquisite mystic informed Korean pottery
        and I won't break them.

 Born in 1923 in Italy, John Tagliabue came to the USA in 1927. After attending public schools in New Jersey he did both undergraduate and graduate work at Columbia University in New York. His professors included the poet Mark Van Doren. In 1945 he was on the first passenger ship (the Gripsholm) to leave New York after the war for Europe and the Middle East. He taught at the American University of Beirut, at State colleges in Pullman, Washington and Alfred, New York before receiving a Fulbright grant to work at the University of Pisa, Italy in 1950. In 1953 John began a long association with Bates College in Lewiston, Maine which lasted until his retirement in 1989. Bates College maintains an archive of John's papers. His love of art and travel took him to many countries often sponsored by Fulbright grants or other foundations. John died in Providence, Rhode Island in 2006.

Books of poetry include:
Poems 1942-1958, Harper Brothers (1959)
A Japanese Journal, Kayak Press (1966)
The Buddha Uproar, Kayak Press (1970)
The Doorless Door, Mushinsha\Grossman (1970)
The Great Day: Poems 1962-1983, The Alambic Press (1984)
New and Selected Poems: 1942-1997
    National Poetry Foundation, (1998)
An Artist in Rome, accompanied by paintings by Adam Van Doren
    Kelly Winterton Press (2009)

Acknowledgements:

We would like to express our appreciation to Bates College in Lewiston, Maine for its support. In addition, there are several people who deserve our gratitude for their invaluable contribution to our project. Amy Webb was responsible for the imaginative and sensitive design of the entire book. We are grateful to Rebecca Szantyr, image coordinator, for her assistance in contacting the many museums represented in the poetry. We also extend our thanks to Nancy Picard, retired Administrative Manager of the Graduate School, Brown University who prepared the original text for publication. Elli Mylonas, Senior Digital Humanities Librarian, Brown University, deserves our gratitude for her guidance in the process of publication.

We would like to thank the following museums and organizations for granting permission to reproduce a selection of specific works of art that inspired the poet. General information about each work of art represented can be found in the text under each image.

AMSTERDAM - Rijksmuseum
REMBRANDT VAN RIJN, *Anatomy Lesson of Dr. Deyman* (page 226)
    Photo Credit: Album / Art Resource, NY
REMBRANDT VAN RIJN, *The Jewish Bride* (page 228)
    Photo Credit: Album / Art Resource, NY
REMBRANDT VAN RIJN, *Jeremiah* (page 230)
    Photo Credit: Album / Art Resource, NY
JOHANNES VERMEER, *The Milkmaid* (page 262)
    Photo Credit: Erich Lessing / Art Resource

AMSTERDAM - Van Gogh Museum
VINCENT VAN GOGH, *The Harvest* (page 258)
    Photo Credit: Snark / Art Resource, NY
VINCENT VAN GOGH, *Landscape with the Chateau of Auvers at Sunset* (page 261)
    Photo Credit: Album / Art Resource, NY
VINCENT VAN GOGH, *Room in Arles* (page 257)
    Photo Credit: Art Resource, NY
VINCENT VAN GOGH, *Yellow House in Arles* (page 255)
    Photo Credit: Art Resource, NY

BOSTON - Summer Street Housing
MARIANNE PINEDA, *Twirling* (278)
    Courtesy Boston Arts Commission, 2014

FLORENCE - Museo Nazionale del Bargello
MICHELANGELO, *Bacchus* (page 202)
    Photo Credit: Scala / Art Resource, NY

FLORENCE - Uffizi Gallery
TITIAN, *Venus of Urbino* (page 246)
    Photo Credit: Scala / Ministero per i Beni e le Attività culturali / Art Resource, NY

THE HAGUE - **Mauritshuis**
CAREL FABRITIUS, *The Goldfinch* (page 182; detail: cover, introduction)
　　Photo Credit: Scala / Art Resource, NY

HARTFORD (CT) - **Wadsworth Atheneum Museum of Art**
PIERRE-AUGUSTE RENOIR, *Monet Painting in Argenteuil* (page 234)
　　Photo Credit: Wadsworth Atheneum Museum of Art / Art Resource, NY

KANSAS CITY (MISSOURI) - **Nelson-Atkins Museum of Art**
VINCENT VAN GOGH, *Olive Orchard* (page 252)
　　Photo Credit: Album / Art Resource, NY

LEWISTON (MAINE) - **Bates College Museum of Art**
MARSDEN HARTLEY, *Untitled /Three Men Standing Behind Women with Aprons*
　　[A study for Fisherman's Family] (page 272)
　　c. 1943, Graphite on white paper, 10 ½ x 8 inches
　　Marsden Hartley Memorial Collection, Bates College Museum of Art,
　　1955.1.96

LONDON - **Courtauld Gallery**
PAUL CÉZANNE, *Lac d'Annecy* (page 176)
　　Photo Credit: Erich Lessing / Art Resource, NY
ÉDOUARD MANET, *Bar at the Folies-Bergere* (page 194)
　　Photo Credit: bpk, Berlin / Courtauld Gallery / Lutz Baum /
　　Art Resource, NY

LONDON - **National Gallery**
PAOLO UCCELLO, *Battle of San Romano* (page 250)
　　© National Gallery, London / Art Resource, NY

LOS ANGELES - **The J. Paul Getty Museum**
REMBRANDT VAN RIJN, *The Abduction of Europa* (page 231)
　　Image reproduced with the permission of The J. Paul Getty Museum,
　　Los Angeles

LOS ANGELES - **Los Angeles County Museum of Art**
MARSDEN HARTLEY, *The Lost Felice* (page 274)
　　Digital Image ©2014 Museums Associates / LACMA.
　　Licensed by Art Resource, NY

MINNEAPOLIS - **Walker Art Center**

Marsden Hartley, *Storm Clouds, Maine* (page 269)
   Collection of the Walker Art Center, Minneapolis
   Gift of the T. B. Walker Foundation, Hudson Walker Collection, 1954

NEW YORK - **Metropolitan Museum of Art**

Jean-Baptiste Camille Corot, *Bacchante by the Sea* (page 128)
   Image copyright © The Metropolitan Museum of Art
   Image source: Art Resource, NY

Giovanni di Paolo, *The Creation* (page 184)
   Image copyright © The Metropolitan Museum of Art
   Image source: Art Resource, NY

Marsden Hartley, *Portrait of a German Officer* (page 270)
   Image Copyright © The Metropolitan Museum of Art
   Image source: Art Resource, NY

Pablo Picasso, *Gertrude Stein* (page 124)
   Image copyright © The Metropolitan Museum of Art
   Image source: Art Resource, NY.
   ©2014 Estate of Pablo Picasso / Artists Rights Society (ARS), New York

Pablo Picasso, *Harlequin* (page 216)
   Image copyright © The Metropolitan Museum of Art
   Image Source: Art Resource, NY.
   ©2014 Estate of Pablo Picasso / Artists Rights Society (ARS), New York

NEW YORK - **Museum of Modern Art**

Piet Mondrian, *Broadway Boogie Woogie* (page 204)
   Digital Image ©The Museum of Modern Art / Licensed by SCALA /
   Art Resource, NY. Reproduced with permission ©2014 Mondrian
   Holtzman Trust c/o HCR International USA

Pablo Picasso, *Les Demoiselles d'Avignon* (page 222)
   Digital Image © The Museum of Modern Art / Licensed by Scala /
   Art Resource, NY.
   ©2014 Estate of Pablo Picasso / Artists Rights Society (ARS), New York

Alfred Stieglitz, *Marsden Hartley* (page 266)
   Digital Image © The Museum of Modern Art
   Licensed by SCALA / Art Resource.
   ©2014 Georgia O'Keeffe Museum / Artists Rights Society (ARS), NY

PARIS - **Musée du Louvre**

CARAVAGGIO, *The Fortune-Teller* (page 36)
> Photo Credit: © RMN-Grand Palais / Art Resource, NY

LEONARDO DA VINCI, *Virgin and Child with Saint Anne* (page 40) (detail: page 41)
> Photo Credit: © RMN-Grand Palais / Art Resource, NY

LEONARDO DA VINCI, *Mona Lisa* (detail: page 43)
> Photo Credit: © RMN-Grand Palais / Art Resource, NY

THÉODORE GÉRICAULT, *The Raft of the Medusa* (page 60)
> Photo Credit: © RMN-Grand Palais / Art Resource, NY

DOMENICO GHIRLANDAIO, *Portrait of an Old Man and a Young Boy* (page 38)
> Photo Credit: Erich Lessing / Art Resource, NY

Unknown Artist, Hellenistic, *The Winged Victory* or *Nike of Samothrace* (page 32)
> Photo Credit: Gianni Dagli Orti/The Art Archive at Art Resource, NY

J. A. D. INGRES, *Oedipus Explains the Riddle of the Sphinx* (page 62)
> Photo Credit: ©RMN-Grand Palais / Art Resource, NY

ANDREA MANTEGNA, Saint Sebastian (page 46)
> Photo Credit: © RMN-Grand Palais / Art Resource, NY

RAPHAEL, *Saint George Fighting the Dragon* (page 48)
> Photo Credit: ©RMN-Grand Palais / Art Resource, NY

REMBRANDT VAN RIJN, *Saint Matthew Inspired by an Angel* (page 52)
> Photo Credit: Erich Lessing / Art Resource, NY

JOHANNES VERMEER, *The Astronomer* (page 56)
> Photo Credit: Erich Lessing / Art Resource, NY

JEAN-ANTOINE WATTEAU, *Pierrot*, also known as *Gilles* (page 64)
> Photo Credit: Erich Lessing / Art Resource, NY

PARIS - **Musée de l'Orangerie**

PIERRE-AUGUSTE RENOIR, *Fraises* (page 90)
> Photo Credit: Erich Lessing / Art Resource, NY

PIERRE-AUGUSTE RENOIR, *Yvonne and Christine Lerolle at the Piano* (page 233)
> Photo Credit: © RMN-Grand Palais / Art Resource, NY

PARIS - **Musée d'Orsay**

PAUL CÉZANNE, *Mont Saint-Victoire* (page 68)
> Photo Credit: ©RMN-Grand Palais / Art Resource, NY

PAUL CÉZANNE, *Still Life with a Soupière* (page 67)
>Photo Credit: Erich Lessing / Art Resource, NY

HENRI DE TOULOUSE-LAUTREC, *The Bed* (page 96)
>Photo Credit: Erich Lessing / Art Resource, NY

PAUL GAUGUIN, *Un Cheval Blanc* (page 76)
>Photo Credit: Erich Lessing / Art Resource, NY

EDOUARD MANET, *Dejeuner sur l'Herbe* (page 80) (detail: cover, preface, page 82)
>Photo Credit: Erich Lessing / Art Resource, NY

ODILON REDON, *La Coquille* (page 87)
>Photo Credit: © RMN-Grand Palais / Art Resource, NY

Henri Rousseau, *La Guerre our La Calvacade de la Discorde* (page 92)
>Photo Credit: RMN-Grand Palais / Art Resource, NY

John Singer Sargent, *La Carmencita* (page 240)
>Photo Credit: Erich Lessing / Art Resource, NY

PARIS - **Musée Picasso**

Pablo Picasso, *Self-Portrait, detail* (page 215)
>Photo Credit: © RMN-Grand Palais / Art Resource, NY
>©2014 Estate of Pablo Picasso / Artists Rights Society (ARS), New York

PARIS - **Musée Rodin**

PIERRE-AUGUSTE RODIN, *Balzac, Nude Study* (page 238)
>Photo Credit: © Vanni Archive / Art Resource, NY

PROVIDENCE - **Museum of Art, Rhode Island School of Design**

Asian; Chinese, *Buddha Head* (cover, page 18)
>Gift of Mrs. Gustav Radeke and Mrs. Jesse H. Metcalf 15.228
>Photography by Erik Gould, courtesy of the Museum of Art,
>Rhode Island School of Design, Providence

GEORGE WESLEY BELLOWS, *Rain on the River* (page 133)
>Jesse Metcalf Fund 15.063
>Photography by Erik Gould, courtesy of the Museum of Art,
>Rhode Island School of Design, Providence

GEORGE BRAQUE, *Still Life* (page 134)
>Mary B. Jackson Fund 48.248
>Photography by Erik Gould, courtesy of the Museum of Art,
>Rhode Island School of Design, Providence

PAUL CÉZANNE, *Au Bord d'une Rivière, Banks of a River* (page 136)
> Museum Special Reserve Fund 43.255
> Photography by Erik Gould, courtesy of the Museum of Art,
> Rhode Island School of Design, Providence

PAUL CÉZANNE, *Still Life with Apples* (Title page) (detail: cover)
> Gift of Mrs. Murray S. Danforth 41.012
> Photography by Erik Gould, courtesy of the Museum of Art,
> Rhode Island School of Design, Providence

THOMAS COLE, *Genesee Scenery* (page 138)
> Jesse Metcalf Fund 38.054
> Photography by Erik Gould, courtesy of the Museum of Art,
> Rhode Island School of Design, Providence

WINSLOW HOMER, *On a Lee Shore* (page 140)
> Jesse Metcalf Fund 01.003
> Photography by Erik Gould, courtesy of the Museum of Art,
> Rhode Island School of Design, Providence

ÉDOUARD MANET, *Le Repos (Repose)* (page 142)
> Bequest of Mrs. Edith Stuyvesant Vanderbilt Gerry 59.027
> Photography by Erik Gould, courtesy of the Museum of Art,
> Rhode Island School of Design, Providence

CLAUDE MONET, *The Seine at Giverny* (page 144)
> Museum Appropriation Fund, by exchange 44.541
> Photography by Erik Gould, courtesy of the Museum of Art,
> Rhode Island School of Design, Providence

THEODORE ROBINSON, *Afternoon Shadows* (page 148)
> Gift of Mrs. Gustav Radeke 20.206
> Photography by Erik Gould, courtesy of the Museum of Art,
> Rhode Island School of Design, Providence

HENRI ROUSSEAU, *Flowers in a Vase* (page 150)
> Gift of Mrs. Murray S. Danforth 42.220
> Photography by Erik Gould, courtesy of the Museum of Art,
> Rhode Island School of Design, Providence

JOHN SINGER SARGENT, *Portrait of Dwight Blaney Sketching* (page 154)
> Gift of Mrs. Houghton P. Metcalf, Sr. 1986.164
> Photography by Erik Gould, courtesy of the Museum of Art,
> Rhode Island School of Design, Providence

Eugene Laurent Vail, *The Grand Canal, Venice* (page 156)
> Museum Collection 49.379
> Photography by Erik Gould, courtesy of the Museum of Art,
> Rhode Island School of Design, Providence

Vincent van Gogh, *View of Arles* (page 158)
> Gift of Mrs. Murray S. Danforth 42.212A
> Photography by Erik Gould, courtesy of the Museum of Art,
> Rhode Island School of Design, Providence

Betty Woodman, *Il Giardino Dipinto*, 1993 (page 282)
> Gift of Charles and Andrea Woodman, Promised gift of Charles and
> Andrea Woodman 2005.110
> Image courtesy of Betty Woodman Estate, with permission of
> Museum of Art, Rhode Island School of Design, Providence

VATICAN STATE, VATICAN PALACE - Sistine Chapel
Michelangelo, *The Creation of Adam* (page 200)
> Photo Credit: Erich Lessing / Art Resource, NY

WASHINGTON, D.C. - National Gallery of Art
Alexander Calder, *Untitled* (page 103)
> Image courtesy National Gallery of Art, Washington, D.C.
> ©2014 Calder Foundation, New York /Artists Rights Society (ARS), NY

Paul Cézanne, *The Artist's Father* (page 104)
> Image courtesy National Gallery of Art, Washington, D.C.

Paul Cézanne, *The Peppermint Bottle* (page 170)
> Image courtesy of the National Gallery of Art, Washington, D.C.

Jean Siméon Chardin, *House of Cards* (detail: page 106)
> Image courtesy of the National Gallery of Art, Washington, D.C.

Jean Siméon Chardin, *Soap Bubbles* (detail: page 107)
> Image courtesy National Gallery of Art, Washington, D.C.

Edgar Degas, *The Dance Lesson* (page 108)
> Image courtesy National Gallery of Art, Washington, D.C.

Henri Matisse, *La Negresse* (page 109)
> Image courtesy National Gallery of Art, Washington, D.C.
> ©2014 Succession H. Matisse / Artists Rights Society (ARS), New York

Claude Monet, *Rouen Cathedral, West Façade* (page 206)
> Image Courtesy of the National Gallery of Art, Washington, D.C.

JOHANNES VERMEER, *A Woman Holding a Balance* (page 112)
    Image courtesy National Gallery of Art, Washington, D.C.
JOHANNES VERMEER, *A Lady Writing* (page 114)
    Image courtesy National Gallery of Art, Washington, D.C.

WASHINGTON, D. C. - **The Phillips Collection**
RAOUL DUFY, *The Artist's Studio,* 1935 (page 117)
        Oil on canvas, 47 x 58 7/8 in. (119.4 x 149.6 cm)
        Acquired 1944, The Phillips Collection, Washington, D.C.
        ©2014 Artists Rights Society (ARS), New York / ADAGP, Paris
HENRI MATISSE, *Studio Quai Saint-Michel,* 1916 (page 118)
        Oil on canvas, 58 ¼ x 46 in. (147.955 x 116.84 cm)
        Acquired 1940, The Phillips Collection, Washington, D. C.
        ©2014 Succession H. Matisse / Artists Rights Society (ARS), New York
JOAN MIRÓ, *The Red Sun*, 1948 (page 120)
        Oil and guache on canvas, 36 1/8 x 28 1/8 in (91.75.75 x 71.4375 cm)
        Acquired 1951, The Phillips Collection, Washington, D.C.
        ©2014 Successió Miró / Artists Rights Society (ARS), New York /
        ADAGP, Paris

CPSIA information can be obtained
at www.ICGtesting.com
Printed in the USA
BVHW070715031119
562764BV00002B/371/P

9 781494 747183